RODALE ORGANIC **GARDENING BASICS**

lawns

**From the Editors of
Rodale Organic Gardening
Magazine and Books**

We're always happy to hear from you. For questions or comments concerning the editorial content of this book, please write to:

Rodale Book Readers' Service
33 East Minor Street
Emmaus, PA 18098

Look for other Rodale books wherever books are sold. Or call us at (800) 848-4735.

For more information about Rodale Organic Gardening magazine and books, visit us at:

www.organicgardening.com

Editor: Karen Costello Soltys
Contributing Editor: Christine Bucks
Interior Book Designer: Nancy Smola Biltcliff
Cover Designer: Patricia Field
Photography Editors: Lyn Horst and
    Lauren Hicks Shelley
Layout Designer: Dale Mack
Researchers: Sarah Wolfgang Heffner,
    Pamela Ruch, and Heidi A. Stonehill
Copy Editors: Christine Bucher and Terry Turner
Manufacturing Coordinator: Mark Krahforst
Indexer: Nan Badgett
Editorial Assistance: Kerrie A. Cadden

RODALE ORGANIC GARDENING BOOKS
Managing Editor: Fern Marshall Bradley
Executive Creative Director: Christin Gangi
Art Director: Patricia Field
Production Manager: Robert V. Anderson Jr.
Studio Manager: Leslie M. Keefe
Associate Copy Manager: Jennifer Hornsby
Manufacturing Manager: Mark Krahforst

Library of Congress
    Cataloging-in-Publication Data
    Rodale organic gardening basics. Lawns /
    from the editors of Rodale Organic Gardening
    Magazine and Books.
        p.   cm.
    Includes bibliographical references (p.   )
    and index.
        ISBN 0-87596-837-6 (pbk. : alk. paper)
        1. Lawns.   2. Organic gardening.
    I. Rodale Books.
    SB433 .075   2000
    635.9'64784—dc21   99-050442

Distributed in the book trade by St. Martin's Press

2   4   6   8   10   9   7   5   3   1   paperback

contents

In Pursuit of the "Perfect" Lawn

We Americans sure do love our lawns. We want our lawn to be greener than our neighbors', lusher than velvet, and weed-free. And wouldn't it be great if it could mow itself, too?

I've got good news for you. You can have a beautiful, green lawn *without* spending hours each week taking care of it and without applying chemical fertilizers and pesticides. That's right, you can have an *organic* lawn, and you'll love it! An organic lawn is lovely and green. It feels wonderful under your bare feet. And you can enjoy watching your children and pets play on it, knowing that it's a completely safe environment for them—and for birds, butterflies, and other wildlife, too.

With this book's basic organic lawn-care techniques, you'll learn how to choose the right grass for your needs, how to apply organic fertilizers, and how to suppress weeds naturally just by changing the way you mow your lawn. I can't promise you a lawn that mows itself (unless you're willing to host a few sheep or goats). But I can promise you that growing an organic lawn is easy and rewarding.

You can enjoy watching your children and pets play on it, knowing that it's a completely safe environment for them.

Happy organic gardening!

Maria Rodale

Maria Rodale

By going organic, you can make your lawn lush, green, and completely safe for child's play.

chapter one

Go Organic: Simplify Your Lawn Care

Contrary to popular belief, it is possible to have a lush, weed-free lawn without using synthetic chemicals. Not only that, once you've made the switch to organic lawn care, you'll find that a chemical-free lawn requires less time and effort to maintain.

ORGANIC = LOW MAINTENANCE

Organic lawns grow more slowly than lawns that are doused with chemical fertilizer, so they don't need to be mowed as often. They also have deeper roots, so they need less watering. Organic lawns can bear all sorts of stress—from excessive heat to drought to heavy foot traffic. Because they're healthier to begin with, organic lawns develop fewer pest and disease problems. And if problems do arise, you can handle them in safe ways that won't harm your family, your pets, or the environment.

> **Organic lawn care allows you to spend less time laboring on your lawn.**

9 THINGS YOU CAN STOP DOING NOW

The first step in switching to organic lawn care is just to *stop* doing many traditional lawn chores. That's right—organic lawn care is not only the best lawn care for the environment, it also allows you to spend less time laboring on your lawn. Less work means more time to spend outside enjoying your lawn: having picnics, playing catch with the kids, gardening, or just enjoying some time to relax. To get you started on your low-maintenance, organic lawn-care program, here are nine things you can stop doing immediately.

1. STOP **Aerating!**

According to the old school of thought, lawns need to be aerated periodically to loosen compacted soil and encourage roots to grow. Aerating means digging small holes in the lawn—using spiky shoes, special rental equipment, or a spading fork—to open up spaces so that oxygen, water, and nutrients can reach grass roots. But most home lawns don't bear enough heavy traffic to cause serious compaction, so they don't need aerating.

In fact, unnecessary aeration can actually *cause* compaction because it introduces too much air into the soil and speeds up decomposition of organic matter (organic matter helps to keep the soil loose and open). The only type of soil that may need periodic aeration is heavy clay soil with low amounts of organic matter—the kind you might find on a new, stripped-down subdivision lot.

2. STOP **Using Chemical Fertilizers!**

Using synthetic fertilizers makes grass grow faster than normal, which means you have to mow more frequently. It also means that earthworms and decomposer organisms won't be able to keep up with all the grass clippings your lawn will produce, and you may end up with a thatch problem. (See number 3 below.) If you want, you can substitute organic fertilizer for chemical fertilizer. For more specifics about organic fertilizers, see "Lawn Maintenance Made Easy," beginning on page 51.

Organic fertilizers are pre-packaged, easy to use, and readily available at most garden centers.

3. STOP **Dethatching!**

Thatch is a layer of undecomposed grass clippings, roots, and other organic matter that can accumulate in lawns; this mass prevents air and water from reaching the soil. Some lawn-care professionals recommend dethatching by machine, but this is not an effective long-term solution to a thatch problem. Excessive thatch is caused by feeding a lawn too much nitrogen, which makes the grass produce leaves, roots, and stems faster than soil organisms can decompose them. Applying pesticides to lawns can also result in thatch buildup because the pesticides also kill earthworms, which are important decomposers of thatch. Without earthworms, thatch buildup is inevitable.

CAN MY LAWN STILL BE NICE AND GREEN?

WHEN YOU FERTILIZE your lawn (about a month after the grass starts growing), you're providing nitrogen, phosphorus, and potassium to the root system. But don't overdo it by trying to create the velvety look of a golf course. Excessive fertilizing can weaken your lawn by causing the grass to grow too quickly. Instead, leave grass clippings on the lawn when you mow, and fertilize just twice a year with a granular organic fertilizer at a reduced rate (cut back by 25 percent from the amount recommended on the label). Your lawn will become healthy and green—without overgrowing. The beauty of organic fertilizers is that they release their nutrients slowly and won't harm the grass or beneficial microorganisms the way chemicals can.

4. STOP **Using Chemical Herbicides!**

Maintaining a 100 percent weed-free lawn by using chemical herbicides is like trying to keep yourself from getting sick by taking antibiotics every day: The problems you'll eventually face from the "cure" will be worse than the occasional illness that might strike! If you douse your lawn with herbicides to keep it weed-free, it may not be a safe place for you, your children, pets, or wildlife to walk or play on. An organic lawn may have a weed in it here and there, but what does that matter?

Instead, let your lawn be its own natural weed-block. This method is a lot healthier for your lawn—and cheaper, too! To battle weeds the natural way, mow your grass often (but not too low) with a sharp blade, don't overfertilize, and build up soil that's rich in organic matter and biological activity.

Planting three or more varieties of grass in a lawn increases the competitiveness of the turf and decreases the chances that weeds will become established. For more weed-control options, see page 65.

Say no to chemical weed killers and bug sprays, and you can rest easy knowing your lawn is a safe place for your kids and pets to romp.

5. STOP **Using Chemical Pesticides!**

All lawns occasionally suffer from insect problems. But applying a pesticide to kill the insects can harm other kinds of soil life—including beneficial earthworms—and make it harder for the grass's natural defenses to overcome the pest invasion. You become caught in a vicious cycle because the pests may come back *stronger* after each application of chemicals, while your lawn keeps getting weaker.

So don't reach for those chemicals—boost your lawn's natural pest-fighting abilities instead. Grass grown in healthy soil has many natural defenses against pests. Some plants, for example, produce their own natural substances that repel or are toxic to pests. For more organic pest-beating options, see page 76.

6. STOP **Overwatering!**

Water is great when you're establishing a new lawn. But if your lawn is more than a couple of years old, hold that hose! Soggy soil deprives grass roots of vital oxygen and encourages diseases that thrive in damp conditions.

Instead of dumping water on your lawn from above, encourage your lawn to retain it below. Building the humus content of your lawn will help the soil hold water (see page 12). Many organically tended lawns thrive without irrigation throughout the growing season because they contain plenty of humus.

To learn how to tell when you really do need to water, see "Lawn Maintenance Made Easy" on page 51. And for another tip on shutting down the sprinkler, see number 7 below.

7. STOP **Mowing Too Short!**

Mowing your lawn very short may make it look like a perfect putting green—but only for a little while. Mowing short will stress your lawn and soon leave it looking brown and scorched. Why? Because grass needs a healthy root mass in order to absorb water and nutrients. When you cut your grass short, the less surface area the grass blades have exposed to the sun. In turn, the grass isn't able to photosynthesize enough food to support good root growth.

The simplest way to help your organic lawn grow up healthy and thick is to adjust your mower's cutting height to its highest setting. Tall blades of grass have

FUN FACT

IT PAYS TO TAKE CARE OF YOUR GRASS ROOTS. AFTER ALL, A SINGLE GRASS PLANT HAS ABOUT 385 MILES OF THEM! THAT MEANS THERE ARE 329,000 MILES OF GRASS ROOTS BELOW EACH SQUARE FOOT OF YOUR LAWN.

----

more surface area exposed to the sun, so they can photosynthesize more easily and produce greater root growth. As a result, the grass can tolerate drought and can recover more rapidly after its dormant period.

Tall grass also outcompetes annual weeds, and it conserves moisture by shading the soil and slowing evaporation from its surface, so the grass needs less watering. For more on mowing height, see "Lawn Maintenance Made Easy" on page 51.

8. STOP Bagging Grass Clippings!

Many people believe that grass clippings left on the lawn contribute to thatch—or they don't like the way clippings look on close-shaved lawns. So these folks bag up the clippings each week and deposit them on the curb to be hauled away.

But just the opposite is true: Fresh clippings stimulate earthworm activity, which breaks down thatch. Clippings also fertilize your lawn. As grass clippings decompose, they contribute valuable nitrogen to the soil—almost 2 pounds of nitrogen per 1,000 square feet of soil each season. (For details, see "Leave the Clippings Where They Fall" on page 54.) When you mow at the right height (see number 7 on page 5), the clippings are hidden in the lawn rather than sticking out as an eyesore. So leave the rake and the grass bagging attachment to your lawn mower in the garage, and let the clippings fall to the ground—and stay there.

9. STOP Treating Your Lawn Like a Golf Course!

Unless you practice putting on your lawn, there's no reason to maintain a golf course in your yard. Many homeowners assume they need a large, manicured lawn because it's what their neighbors have. Set aside that assumption, and the possibilities for transforming your lawn are nearly endless.

---

quick tip

Grass clippings contain approximately 4 percent nitrogen, 2 percent potassium, and 0.5 percent phosphorus—a great all-around natural fertilizer for your lawn. And what could be easier than leaving them right where they fall? You won't have to add purchased fertilizer or waste time raking them up.

In heavy traffic areas, such as children's play areas and the spot for your picnic table, consider mulch instead of grass. It's soft underfoot, and you won't have to worry about compacting the soil, damaging the turf, or mowing around structures.

Spend some time thinking about your yard and how you use it. Perhaps you or your children like to play lots of active games and sports outside. If so, you'll probably want to maintain a fairly large area of open lawn. If you use your yard primarily for summer meals and parties, you may want to enlarge your patio or deck and surround it with easy-to-maintain flowering groundcovers instead of a lawn. That way you'll have more free time for entertaining and a more attractive setting for your gatherings, too.

Your yard can also be a place to relax and unwind as well as to watch birds and other wild creatures. If that's how you'd like to spend time in your yard, consider converting some of your lawn to flower borders or hedges to increase privacy and to provide better habitat for wildlife. You can also add beauty and color to your yard by converting some of your yard to plantings of flowering trees, shrubs, and perennials. To learn more about the terrific potential of nongrass lawns, check out "Beyond the Traditional Lawn" on page 79.

In healthy soil there will be plenty of worms busy at work decomposing grass clippings—even enough to share with the early birds.

chapter two

Start with the Soil

Healthy soil—fertile, well drained, and free of pests and diseases—is the foundation for a healthy lawn. Analyzing the health of your soil may sound tricky, but in this chapter you'll learn how to use nature's clues to help you understand your soil and what it needs to grow better grass.

WHAT IS SOIL?

Just what is soil and what does it do? Soil is made up of minerals, organic matter, water, and air. Without sufficient amounts of each, grass just won't grow.

Soil is constantly being formed by the same forces that created it originally—climate and decaying plant matter. Plants decompose to provide organic matter to the soil, and roots break it down into smaller particles. In turn, the soil provides support and nutrients for plants. But when things get out of whack and there's not enough air space (compaction) or the right amount of water (poor drainage), or minerals and organic matter are missing, you can have real problems growing grass—or any other plants, for that matter.

In this chapter you'll learn the basics of how to tell how healthy your soil is—both by soil testing and from the signs Mother Nature provides. You'll also learn how to fix common soil problems so you can enjoy your ideal lawn.

SIZING UP YOUR LAWN

You can tell a lot about the health of your lawn (and the soil it's growing in) simply by taking a good look at it. The best time to do this is when the grass is growing vigorously—a few days after the second mowing of the season. Here's what to do:

Soil is made of minerals, organic matter, water, and air. Without them, grass just won't grow.

Your lawn can tell you a lot about your soil's condition, if you know what to look for. Too much thatch can mean a soil compaction problem (above). A lawn full of clover (below) indicates that more nitrogen is needed.

Decide whether your grass has good color. Healthy lawn grass is a moderate green. Faded green grass, with brown-and-green blades, indicates moisture, disease, or soil fertility problems.

Check for a hefty layer of turf. The turf should be thick enough so that you can't see the soil peeking through it. (If you can see bare soil, there's room for weeds to invade your lawn.)

Size up thatch thickness. Thatch is the buildup of grass roots and stems that sits on the surface of the soil. In general, less than ½ inch of thatch isn't a problem. However, when thatch is more than ½ inch thick, it may block water, air, and fertilizer from reaching the soil. This in turn will stress the grass, making it more susceptible to disease. Pest insects can hide in thick thatch, too.

Study the weeds. Look at how many weeds you have, where they are growing, and what they are. These are clues to healthy or sickly soil. Here's a list of common weeds and what they may be telling you:

● Lots of clover in your lawn could mean your soil is low in nitrogen.

- Plantain indicates heavy, poorly drained soil (lawns don't like constantly wet conditions).
- Mosses are found in acidic sites (many lawn grasses don't grow well in acid soil).
- Clumps of weeds may mean your soil is compacted.

WHAT'S GOING ON *BELOW* THE GRASS

Once you've taken a look at what's happening on top of your lawn, it's time to move below ground. To scope things out down under, try these easy tests.

The root test. Set up a sprinkler on your lawn and run it for an hour. Then wait 15 minutes and, using a sharp knife, cut out a sample of sod and soil about 6 inches wide and 6 inches deep. Carefully lift the section out and turn it over. If the roots of your grass only extend into the first 2 inches of soil, your lawn probably has a soil compaction problem. If your lawn grass roots extend 4 to 6 inches deep and water has penetrated all the way to the bottom of the sample, hooray!—you have loose, well-drained soil that will support a healthy lawn.

The watering test. Two days after a thorough watering (at least 1 inch of water), dig a small, 6-inch-deep hole in an area where you watered. If the soil is already dry all the way to the bottom of the hole, your soil probably drains too rapidly and won't retain enough water for healthy lawn growth.

The compaction test. Stick a screwdriver into the soil in several places. If you have trouble pushing the blade in up to the handle, your soil has a compaction problem.

The earthworm/grub test. Dig up a cubic foot of soil and spread it out on a tarp or newspaper. Look through the soil and count the earthworms you find. Soil that's reasonably moist and at least 55°F should

Deep grass roots are a sign of healthy soil and healthy grass.

Test for water retention in your soil by digging a hole in your lawn to see how quickly a heavy watering has drained away.

White grubs, the larvae of Japanese beetles, reside in the soil, eating grass roots. If you have too many in your grass, you'll have a problem maintaining a healthy lawn.

have an earthworm population of at least ten earthworms per cubic foot. If your earthworm count is low, it may mean that there's not enough organic matter in your soil, that your soil is too acidic or alkaline, or that it has a mineral imbalance.

While you're counting earthworms, take a grub count as well. If you find more than five grubs per cubic foot, you have a grub problem. (See "Grubs, Bugs, and a Rodent or Two" on page 74 for directions on how to get rid of grubs.)

FUN FACT

Earthworms, the helpful heroes of the soil, are naturally long-lived—up to 15 years, depending on the species. However, with robins and all the other dangers of the natural world, few make it to old age. Earthworms want to make sure they stick around, so they multiply at the amazing rate of 2,000 to 3,000 offspring each year per worm! (And, of course, they also re-grow when cut in half.)

FIXING WHAT YOU FIND

If you discover problems with your soil, such as compaction or poor drainage, how do you fix them? After all, digging up your whole lawn to fix the soil underneath just isn't practical. What is practical, and very effective, is putting compost on *top* of your lawn. That's right: Spreading organic matter such as compost or well-rotted manure on your lawn will actually help to solve underlying soil problems.

Compost Equals More Earthworms

When you spread organic matter on your lawn with a rake, it will eventually settle to the soil surface, where it will boost earthworm populations and activity (remember, earthworms eat organic matter). All the tunneling by earthworms opens up more spaces in the soil for water to drain through. This is especially true if you have heavy clay soil with poor drainage.

Compost Improves Drainage

Adding compost also improves the water-holding capacity of sandy soils because compost can retain lots

of moisture. It's the best quick fix you can give your soil. In the fall, add 1 to 2 inches of organic compost (along with any organic fertilizers your soil test indicated you need—see "Get a Professional Soil Test" below), and work it all into the soil with a rake. For more details on adding compost, see "Lawn Maintenance Made Easy" on page 51.

Raking compost into your lawn will lead to healthier soil below. As it decomposes, the compost improves drainage and alleviates compaction problems.

GET A PROFESSIONAL SOIL TEST

While the do-it-yourself tests described above will indicate if you have compacted soil, grubs, or other soil problems, there's another kind of test you'll want to have done. It's simply called a soil test, and it's one of the best things you can do for your lawn. The test results will tell you the pH level of your soil and whether it needs a little more of one nutrient or a little less of another.

A soil test may seem expensive or daunting, but it's really not. All you do is collect a sample of your soil and send it to a testing service. In fact, you can

quick tip

How do you know if you have sandy or clay soil? Dig up a shovelful of soil from your yard and rub a pinch between your fingers. Clay soil feels hard when dry and slippery when wet. Sandy soil is gritty. Compost will help improve drainage for both soil types.

A soil sample for testing is easy to prepare with the help of a special kit, and the results will determine exactly what you need to feed your grass and soil.

Collect soil from a few different spots to get a more accurate, overall reading of what's going on below your lawn.

probably have your soil tested through your local cooperative extension office for around $10 (you can find the number for the extension office in your telephone book). If you call the extension office, they'll tell you where and how to buy a soil collection kit locally.

Once you have the kit, simply follow the instructions for taking a soil sample (see "Collecting Soil" below for a few hints), mail the sample in, and wait for the results and recommendations.

Collecting Soil

To collect a soil sample, you'll need a spade, a trowel, a knife, and a bucket.

1. Using the spade, cut the sod from an area of your lawn. Then cut and lift out a wedge-shaped piece of soil rougly 6 to 8 inches deep. Set the soil and the sod aside.

2. Use the spade to slice a ½-inch-thick piece of soil from the smooth side of the hole.

3. With the slice resting on the spade, use the knife to cut off both ends of the slice, leaving a 1-inch core in the center. Put the core in the bucket.

4. Put the remaining soil back into the hole and tamp the sod back into place.

5. Repeat Steps 1 through 3 about a half-dozen times in different parts of your lawn, then use your trowel to mix the samples together in the bucket.

6. Fill the soil sample bag that came in the kit with some of this mixture, fill out the accompanying paperwork, and send it all off to the lab.

The Great Lime Debate

If your neighbor diligently applies lime to his lawn every year, you may think you ought to be doing the same. But wait a minute before you head out to buy that lime! Your lawn (and your neighbor's) may not need lime at all—and if it doesn't, why go to the time and expense?

The only way to really know whether your lawn needs lime is to test your soil. The test results will include the pH, a measurement of the soil's acidity or alkalinity. If your soil is too acidic (a pH below 6.5), the report recommendations will probably suggest you add lime to raise the pH.

Which kind of lime you apply will depend on another portion of the test results: the magnesium level. If your soil's magnesium levels are acceptable, the recommendation is usually to add calcitic lime. When soil needs a magnesium boost, however, adding dolomitic lime (also called magnesium lime) can correct both problems at the same time.

If your soil's pH is above 7.0, it's on the alkaline side and you won't want to add lime at all!

Lots of homeowners spread lime on their lawns, but it's only a good idea if your soil test results indicate that your soil is acidic. If you have neutral or alkaline soil, you could do more harm than good. So always test the soil first.

Before you scoop out a bag full of grass seed, it pays to investigate which types of grass will grow best where you live.

chapter three

Choosing the Right Grass

Whether you're getting ready to install a new lawn or are thinking of revitalizing your old one, don't buy the first grass seed you find on sale at your local garden center. The area where you live determines the specific types of turfgrass that will thrive. Planting one of these grasses now will save you a lot of effort later. Growing the right grass makes it easy to keep your lawn healthy, vigorous, and relatively weed-free.

SOME LIKE IT HOT, SOME LIKE IT COOL

The guidelines in this chapter will help you choose the grass that's best for your lawn. Keep in mind that the type of grass you should plant not only varies by region but also within specific regions. Read about the grasses recommended for your region on the following pages.

Turfgrasses are divided into two different groups: cool-season grasses and warm-season grasses. Cool-season grasses grow best when temperatures are between 60° and 75°F. Warm-season grasses grow best at a sultry 80° to 95°F. The one exception is a turfgrass called buffalograss that grows well in either warm or cool conditions as long as humidity is low.

As you might expect, cool-season grasses grow best in the northern part of the United States. How far south they can grow and still look good depends on how hot it will get during the summer. Warm-season grasses, on the other hand, grow best in the Southeast and Southwest. How far north they can be grown depends on how low the temperatures dip in an area during the winter.

> **Growing the right grass makes it easy to keep your lawn healthy, vigorous, and weed-free.**

Identify your grass zone on the map to pick the right kind of grass to grow in your backyard. The area outlined with a dotted line represents the transition zone (see the opposite page).

Preferred temperatures aren't the only difference between cool- and warm-season grasses. Cool-season grasses retain their green color during the cooler times of the year, even in winter. Warm-season grasses will lose their color and go dormant following a frost.

WHAT'S YOUR GRASS ZONE?

The United States has been divided into five "grass zones" based on temperature and rainfall. Locate your state on the map (above), then read on to see which types of turfgrass are suited to your zone.

ZONE 1: THE NORTHEAST. Good grasses for this region include Kentucky bluegrass, Chewings fescues, turf-type tall fescues, and perennial ryegrass.

ZONE 2: THE SOUTH. Bermudagrass, zoysiagrass, bahiagrass, centipedegrass, and St. Augustinegrass all grow well in the hot and humid South. All of these grasses except centipedegrass are recommended for Hawaiian lawns, too.

ZONE 3: THE GREAT PLAINS. The choices in this region are between Kentucky bluegrass, turf-type tall fescue, and low-maintenance buffalograss.

ZONE 4: THE SOUTHWEST. The grass you choose should depend on your elevation.

- **Low elevations:** Bermudagrass is a good choice for its tolerance to heat, stress, and poor soil conditions.

- **High elevations:** Cool-season grasses such as Kentucky bluegrass, fescues, and perennial ryegrass are better choices.

- **California:** You can grow cool- or warm-season grasses successfully from the San Francisco Bay area to Southern California, but cool-season grasses have the advantage of staying green year-round.

ZONE 5: THE NORTHWEST. Cool-season grasses, such as Kentucky bluegrass, fescues, and perennial ryegrass, grow best in this humid region, but choose your grass based on where you live.

- **East of the Cascades:** Try a mix of Kentucky bluegrass and perennial ryegrass or fescues.

- **West of the Cascades:** Grow perennial ryegrass mixed with another species like fine fescue or a variety of Kentucky bluegrass.

- **Alaska:** Try planting Kentucky bluegrass or some of the fine fescues in Alaska.

THE TRANSITION ZONE

AREAS WHERE neither cool- nor warm-season grasses grow very well—humid parts of the Southeast and Midwest—are called the "transition zone." The boundaries of this zone are indicated on the map on the opposite page.

If you live in the transition zone, you may have a more difficult time growing a lush and lovely lawn than folks in other regions. The climate changes from year to year in transition zone areas, making it particularly difficult to have a healthy, vigorous lawn. Because no single turfgrass is well adapted to this changing climate, weeds have an easy time getting a foothold.

Your best bet is to plant either a cold-tolerant, warm-season grass, such as zoysiagrass, or a heat-tolerant, cool-season grass, such as Kentucky bluegrass or improved turf-type tall fescue.

COOL-SEASON GRASSES

All turfgrasses have their strong points and short-comings. Now that you've figured out whether warm- or cool-season grasses are best for where you live, the following pictures and descriptions about the specific choices should help you decide which type of grass or grasses is best for your lawn needs.

KENTUCKY BLUEGRASS

Kentucky bluegrass (*Poa pratensis*) is a lush, dark green grass with narrow blades that form a dense turf—the envy of the neighborhood!

Buying a named variety of Kentucky bluegrass assures your grass seed has been selected to produce specific, high-quality traits. So don't buy plain old Kentucky bluegrass.

- Is the most commonly used grass in cool, humid regions

- Doesn't grow well in hot spots like Florida

- Its spreading habit forms sod quickly.

- Over 100 "named" varieties have been selected for quality attributes such as shade tolerance, thick turf, and so on. Look for one to suit your needs.

PERENNIAL RYEGRASS

Perennial ryegrass (*Lolium perenne*) is a medium-textured, spreading grass that bounces back from wear. A good choice for picnics, volleyball, and croquet.

Perennial ryegrass has a coarser texture than Kentucky blue-grass, but it also has many desirable traits. Mix it with bluegrass for a beautiful, trouble-free lawn.

- Germinates rapidly

- Outcompetes weeds

- Doesn't produce as much thatch as other grasses

- Is good for high-traffic areas—very wear-tolerant

- Choose endophyte-containing seed for a naturally pest-repellent lawn (see "Endo-phyte Grasses Fight Pests" on page 75).

-- FINE FESCUES ----------------------->

Fine fescues (*Festuca* spp.) are dark green, fine-textured grasses that include creeping red, Chewings, and hard fescues. Red fescue is a sod-forming perennial. Chewings fescue is a bunch grass that's more erect and doesn't spread by rhizomes. Hard fescue is a nonspreading bunch grass.

- Tolerates shade
- Tolerates drought better than other cool-season grasses
- Is low maintenance
- Emerges from summer dormancy better than most grasses

Red fescue is a perfect choice for a shady lawn, whether you're starting from scratch or overseeding an existing lawn.

-- TURF-TYPE TALL FESCUE ------------->

Regular tall fescue was originally bred for animals to graze on, but turf-type tall fescue (*Festuca arundinacea*) is a coarse, medium green grass that has been developed specifically for lawns.

- Is tough enough for high traffic areas
- Has the potential to develop the deep root system needed for drought tolerance
- Becomes stressed when mowed too short
- Stays rich and green without high doses of nitrogen—low maintenance

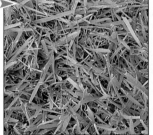

If long, dry summers can be a problem in your area, then turf-type tall fescue might be for you.

BUFFALOGRASS

BUFFALOGRASS (*Buchloe halides*) is not specifically a warm- or cool-season grass, but a true prairie grass (it grows naturally in the Central Plains). It does well in cool or warm temperatures, but it doesn't like humidity and moisture. It's a good choice for lawns in dry areas from Texas and Oklahoma north into Canada.

WARM-SEASON GRASSES

BERMUDAGRASS

Bermudagrass (*Cynodon dactylon*) is a vigorous grower that is often used as a "sports grass" in areas such as high-maintenance golf fairways.

- Tolerates drought very well
- Stands up to heat and high traffic
- Won't tolerate shade very well
- Needs to be mowed frequently—high maintenance
- Hybrid bermudagrasses, which have finer leaf blades than the common type, are only available as sod or plugs.

Planting bermudagrass can mean beautiful Southern lawns, but there is a trade-off— bermudagrass needs to be mowed frequently.

ZOYSIAGRASS

Zoysiagrasses (*Zoysia* spp.) are slow-growing grasses that are primarily grown in the South but also grow well in some cool-season or transition-zone areas. Blades may be coarse to fine, depending upon the species.

- Is slow-growing, which means less frequent mowing
- Is wear-resistant
- Dense sod chokes out weeds.
- Forms shallow roots, so needs irrigation in dry areas
- Produces thatch that needs to be raked
- The best species for cooler areas is *Zoysia japonica,* which is also called Japanese or Korean lawn grass.

Zoyziagrass forms a nice thick sod that stays green all summer long, but it turns straw-colored at the first sign of cold.

-- ST. AUGUSTINEGRASS ----------------------

St. Augustinegrass (*Stenotaphrum secundatum*) is a coarse-textured, sod-forming perennial grass for the mid-South.

- Tolerates shade
- Grows best along southern coast of the United States; suffers from winterkill in other areas
- Requires fertile soil, rich in organic matter
- Needs good soil drainage
- Doesn't set viable seed; need to establish from sod or plugs
- You need to keep mower blades sharp to mow it.

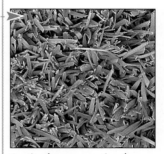

One of the best grasses for coastal regions, St. Augustine-grass loves the good drainage of sandy soils. It can be touchy to grow elsewhere.

-- CENTIPEDEGRASS ----------------------

Centipedegrass (*Eremochloa ophiuroides*) is a medium-coarse, sod-forming perennial grass that speads rapidly by creeping stems called stolons, which is how the grass got its name.

- Is best low-maintenance grass for the Deep South
- Grows in poor soils and acid soils
- Dense, vigorous turf is resistant to weed invasion.
- Needs less watering, fertilizing, and mowing than other warm-season grasses
- Needs mowing only every 10 to 20 days
- Expensive per pound, but the seed is so small that you get a lot of seed for your money.

Centipedegrass promises low maintenance for the home-owner who plants it. Just make sure you live in the South or it won't survive the winter!

Don't be overwhelmed by a vast expanse of barren soil if you've just purchased a new home. You can easily turn bare ground into a lush oasis by sowing seed, laying sod, or hiring a hydroseeding contractor.

chapter four

Starting a New Lawn

If you're the owner of a brand-new home, you're probably moving into a lovely new house surrounded by a "yard" of bare soil. You may wonder how you'll ever turn that barren landscape into a beautiful lawn and gardens. In this chapter, you'll learn how to get the grass growing fast, the organic way.

INVESTIGATE YOUR OPTIONS

One big decision to make when you're starting a new lawn is whether to sow grass seed or lay sod. This chapter will explain the pros and cons of both methods and guide you through each, so that when the time comes, you can easily do it yourself.

While laying sod and sowing seed are the two most popular methods for starting a lawn, hydroseeding is another option you might want to consider. If you've never heard of this state-of-the-art technique and you're curious, turn to page 32 to learn more about hydroseeding and how it's done.

Help for Old Lawns, Too

Sometimes existing lawns need a "restart." If your established lawn has bare spots, unwanted weeds, or is otherwise in need of a face-lift, turn to "Reseeding an Existing Lawn" on page 32. You'll learn how you can have a new lawn—without ripping up the old one—by overseeding it with a new grass. But first, you'll need to decide if your old lawn is worth over-seeding. If it's more than 50 percent good grass, you can repair it with overseeding. But if you have more weeds than grass, the lawn is probably not worth trying to save. In the long run, it's easiest to dig it up and start over.

> **One big decision to make when you're starting a new lawn is whether to sow grass seed or lay sod.**

Newly seeded grass won't have a thick, lush appearance immediately, but it's easier for a lawn grown from seed to establish a nice, deep root system.

THE PROS AND CONS OF SEEDING AND SODDING

No method of installing a new lawn is perfect—each has advantages and disadvantages. Knowing what they are will help you make the best decision for your situation.

Seed Pros

- Many different grass varieties are available by seed.
- Seeding leads to strong initial root development.
- Grass seed is much less expensive than sod.

Seed Cons

- A thick lawn takes longer to establish.
- There's a limited window of opportunity for planting.
- Weeds compete with grass seed.
- Seed is hard to plant and water on slopes.

While you still have to prepare your soil surface before you can lay sod, it doesn't take long to roll out the sod into a fabulous new lawn.

Sod Pros

- Sod creates an instant weed-free lawn.
- You can sod a lawn at any time during the growing season.
- Grass establishes easily on slopes and in other areas prone to erosion.

Sod Cons

- Sod is expensive, especially with installation.
- Your choice of grasses is limited with sod.
- Sod rolls must be kept wet until they are laid.

PREPARING THE SITE

Whether you choose to start your lawn from seed or sod, be prepared to spend more time preparing your planting area than on the planting itself. Because you *really* don't want to start a lawn more than once, it's important to do what it takes to provide good, healthy soil that will sustain your grass indefinitely.

Clean Up New Sites

If you're starting with a site that still shows the aftermath of construction work, begin by removing rocks and debris. Then rough-grade the area to eliminate drainage problems. If you're lucky enough to have a clear, properly graded site, you can skip the cleanup.

To start a new lawn right, the first step is to remove all rocks, twigs, and old sod from the soil, and rake the surface smooth with a garden rake.

Strip Old Lawns

You may be renovating an old lawn rather than starting a brand-new one. Your first step will be to get rid of the old sod and weeds. You can rent a sod stripper to slice this top layer, or hire someone to do it for you. Don't throw the removed sod out with the trash. It takes some time to break down, but if you add it to your compost pile now, you can use it in next year's garden.

Test for Success

Don't forget to test your soil for pH level and nutrient deficiencies. The results will tell you whether you need to add amendments to adjust your soil's pH. (Refer to "Get a Professional Soil Test" on page 13 for information on soil testing and pH.)

quick tip

The best soil for turfgrass is loam (soil that contains a balance of fine clay, medium-size silt, and coarse sand particles) or sandy loam with a pH of 6.0 to 7.0. For low-care growth, the depth of the topsoil should ideally be 6 inches. The closer your conditions come to the ideal, the easier it will be for you to maintain a dense, deeply rooted, water-efficient lawn.

Before sodding or seeding, roll the surface to get out any bumps or dips. Use a light roller so you don't inadvertently compact the soil.

quick tip

You don't need to buy a rotary tiller or a roller just to prepare your new lawn. Many equipment rental shops have these tools on hand. Since you'll only prepare your new lawn site once, save the expense of buying equipment and put the dollars you save toward your seed or sod and soil amendments.

Till the Soil

Now you're ready to work the soil. Till the soil at least 2 inches deep (and 4 inches is even better). If you discover that part or all of your yard has either heavy clay soil or sandy soil, add topsoil and compost—the more the better—and till to incorporate them. Amazingly, compost helps improve the texture and drainage of both sandy and clay soils.

Then rake your yard smooth, roll the area with a light lawn roller, and allow it to settle for a week or so. Rain or watering with a sprinkler will help it settle.

SHOPPING FOR SEED

Buying grass seed can be a tricky business. One thing that helps is learning to interpret the labels on bags and boxes of grass seed. All labels list the amount of five things that might be in the bag or box.

Turfgrass is first and is listed as a percentage. There may be one or more species with several varieties of each. They must be listed as fine- or coarse-textured.

"Other ingredients" refers to three items that may or may not be in your grass seed—weed seed, inert matter, and crop seeds—listed in percentages.

Noxious weeds, as determined by your state agriculture department, are listed separately, by numbers of seeds per pound.

Interpreting the Labels

What do these numbers mean to your future lawn?

Noxious weeds can include wild garlic, plantain, and annual bluegrass—weeds that spread quickly and are hard to get rid of. Top-quality grass seed will contain *no* noxious weed seed.

Crop seed can be even more troublesome than noxious weeds. These plants usually aren't considered weeds—until they turn up in a lawn. Timothy, orchard grass, and bentgrass are examples. Look for a mix that contains well below 1 percent of crop seed.

Inert matter includes chaff, hulls, stones, and such, and all seed contains a bit of it. It won't harm your lawn, but it's a waste of your money to pay for seed that's more than 3 percent inert matter.

Turfgrasses are listed in descending order by the percent present in the mixture. The germination percentage of each should be listed, too.

quick tip

About ¾ of a cubic yard of compost or topsoil will cover 1,000 square feet of lawn at ½ inch thick. So to add 1 inch to the same size area, you'd need twice as much, or 1½ cubic yards.

```
FALL SPECIAL LAWN SEED MIXTURE        TESTED:AUGUST 1999
NET WGT 3.00      POUNDS (1.358 KG)  LOT NO.:48-29970.X23
       PURE SEED                     ORIGIN GERMINATION
34.48%BARON KENTUCKY BLUEGRASS           WA    85%
24.84%STATESMAN II  PERENNIAL RYEGRASS   OR    95%
14.60%CREEPING RED FESCUE *              CAN   85%
14.57%ECLIPSE KENTUCKY BLUEGRASS         WA    85%
 9.85%CHEWINGS FESCUE *                  OR    85%

OTHER COMPONENTS:
 0.00%  CROP SEED
 1.64%  INERT MATTER      *VARIETY NOT STATED
 0.02%  WEED SEED
NOXIOUS WEED SEED PER POUND:      IBM NO: 548654
NONE
```

Look closely at the label on the grass seed package before you buy so you know exactly what you're getting.

Recommended Mixes for Typical Conditions

When you shop for grass seed, keep the seed ingredients in mind—and consider your yard's conditions. A shady lawn, for instance, won't offer the same growing conditions as a lawn in full sun. To get you started, here are a few mixes and blends suited to typical conditions such as shade, drought, and so on.

BUY QUALITY SEED

WHEN YOU BUY grass seed, be sure to purchase a "named" (certified) variety to be assured of quality. For example, a named variety's label will indicate that it contains 'America' Kentucky bluegrass rather than just Kentucky bluegrass. Certified seed has been inspected and is true to type. If available, look for packages that say "improved" named varieties.

On the other hand, avoid seed with the letters "VNS" (which stands for "variety not stated") on the package. If you buy a VNS product, you don't know what you'll end up with. It's worth spending the extra money to get a specific variety; after all, a lawn should last 20 to 30 years. So the additional cost over the life of that lawn is truly negligible.

Another warning: If you're looking for a *permanent* turf cover, be sure the seed you're buying doesn't contain *any* annual ryegrass (which is different than the *perennial* ryegrass recommended for cool-season lawns).

For more specifics about each type of grass, see "Choosing the Right Grass" on page 17.

- A good general-purpose turfgrass for cool-region lawns is a mix of named Kentucky bluegrass (not common Kentucky bluegrass) and red fescue.

- For shade, a mix should include more fescue than bluegrass. A good blend would be a mix of 40 percent named Kentucky bluegrass, 40 percent red fescue, and 20 percent perennial ryegrass.

- For high-traffic shady lawns, plant 95 percent turf-type tall fescue with 5 percent Kentucky bluegrass.

- For open, sunny locations, use equal amounts of improved red fescue and improved Kentucky bluegrass.

STARTING A LAWN FROM SEED

Early fall, when the soil is still warm but the air temperatures are cooler than in summer, is the best time to plant cool-season grasses in the North. Annual weeds are dying back and won't compete with tender grass seedlings as they would in spring. Newly sprouted grass plants that are six to eight weeks old before the first hard frost should easily survive winter.

In the South, it's a different story. Many weed seeds germinate in the fall, and grasses sown then will face stiff competition from winter annual weeds such as chickweed, henbit, and speedwell. The best time to sow a southern lawn is in the spring or early summer.

1. Last-Chance Soil Prep

By the time you're ready to seed, your lawn area should be leveled, tilled, and raked. This is your last chance to see that the planting surface is smooth—a rough surface means a bumpy lawn. Use a garden rake to scratch shallow furrows into the soil (no more than ½ inch deep) before spreading the seed.

2. Spread the Seed

If you're sowing a small area, seeding with a handheld broadcast spreader is an easy way to go. Otherwise, use a drop-type fertilizer spreader. Calibrate the spreader to the rate that is listed on the grass seed bag. (For more on spreaders, see "Spreaders" on page 49.)

After seeding, rake the soil lightly to barely cover the seed. Then firm the seeded area by rolling it lightly with a lawn roller, or tamping with the back of a rake.

When seeding, it's best to make two applications. Sow half the seed in one direction, and sow the second half at a right angle to the first to ensure even distribution of seed.

3. Add Water!

Once your grass seed begins to germinate, it needs constant moisture. Tiny grass seedlings will quickly die if they dry out.

Don't allow the soil surface to dry out until the grass is 2 inches tall. Sprinkle it lightly but often (at least once a day—twice a day if the weather is very hot and dry). Mulch lightly with weed-free straw (not hay, which contains weed seeds) to retain moisture and keep the grass seed in place. Floating row covers (a sheet of synthetic fabric that lets light and water through) also provide excellent protection for newly seeded areas. Simply cover the new lawn area with the fabric and pin it in place with landscape staples.

Remove row covers or straw after the seeds have germinated so the young plants won't smother. To remove straw, rake it off gently with a leaf rake.

When your lawn reaches a height of 3 to 4 inches, it's time to mow. Now your lawn will benefit from less frequent, deeper watering.

A light layer of straw tossed over your newly sown lawn will help improve the germination rate: It keeps the seed in place, protects it from birds, and retains moisture.

More and more lawns at new construction sites are being seeded quickly and easily with a process called hydroseeding. Grass seed, mulch, fertilizer, and water are all spewed from a hose at one time, making quick work of seeding big lawns.

HYDROSEEDING

Just what is hydroseeding? Hydroseeding involves applying a mixture of grass seed, water, fertilizer, and a biodegradable fiber mulch. The fiber mulch can be made of wood, paper, or a blend of the two. Paper mulch, if applied too heavily, can form a crust that will smother the germinating seeds.

Why Hydroseed?

With hydroseeding, the grass seed, fertilizer, and mulch are applied all in one step, so the process is much quicker than conventional seeding. The fiber mulch is weed-free, protects the seed from birds and rodents, and provides good erosion control on slopes. The mixture helps to retain the warmth and moisture needed for rapid seed germination. All these benefits add up to a considerable advantage when establishing a lawn in a large or hard-to-reach area.

Hydroseeding does have a drawback, of course—it's applied professionally so it may cost a lot more than spreading seed yourself. But if your budget can stretch that far, hydroseeding is a great option.

RESEEDING AN EXISTING LAWN

Overseeding is a good choice if your whole lawn simply looks ragged, or if you want to switch over to one or more of the new, low-maintenance grasses that are resistant to pests and diseases. Or maybe you just don't like the look of your grass. If you have a coarse species that looks rough and weedy compared to your neighbor's grass, overseeding can improve your lawn easily.

quick tip

When you're looking for a landscaper to hydroseed your lawn, be sure to ask if they can include *organic* fertilizer in your mix.

1. Prepare the Turf

If you're dealing with a small area—1,000 square feet or less—the only tools you need for overseeding are a heavy metal garden rake and a lawn mower.

- First mow the lawn closely, at half the normal mowing height and as low as ½ inch, depending on the species.

- Rake the lawn thoroughly. Remove all clippings and as much thatch as possible, to expose a good deal of soil. Pull, cut, or hoe out any weeds.

- Rake the lawn one more time to rough up the soil and give the new seed a place to take root.

For larger areas, it pays to rent a verticutter or slice seeder at a tool rental shop. The verticutter is like a lawn mower with blades set on end. It slices through thatch and soil, making a good environment for grass seed to germinate. Run the machine over the entire area in one direction, then run it over the lawn again in a direction perpendicular to the first. Then you're ready to seed. A slice seeder will cut the sod and sow the seed in one operation.

2. Sow the Seed

Because you'll be sowing seed over an area that already has some sod, not all the seed will come in contact with the soil, so you won't get as high a germination rate. To compensate for this, use 1½ times the amount of seed recommended on the seed package. For example, if perennial ryegrass should usually be spread at a rate of 4 to 6 pounds per 1,000 square feet, you'll overseed it at 6 to 9 pounds.

- Use a drop spreader, or toss the seed by hand in wide arcs as you walk slowly over the area.

- After sowing, go over the area once again with the garden rake, lightly this time.

OVERSEEDING IN THE SOUTH

IN THE SOUTH, you can over-seed a cool-season grass over warm-season grass in the fall to have winter color. Some people overseed annually to keep their lawns green year-round.

For best results, overseed a bermudagrass lawn with blue-grass, perennial ryegrass, or annual ryegrass. Results are not good over zoysiagrass. In late August or September, clip the grass to 1 inch high or shorter. Rake the lawn thoroughly with a heavy metal garden rake. Then sow the overseeded grass at 1½ times the normal rate. Continue mowing at a height of 1 inch until the bermudagrass stops growing, usually by the end of October. Then raise the mower height to 2 inches, and mow when the grass reaches 3 inches. Mow at this height through the winter. In summer, as the cool-season grass goes dormant, the warm-season grass will take over again.

● For best results, top-dress the area with a thin layer of sand or topsoil. You only need about ½ cubic yard per 1,000 square feet.

● Water the lawn well, putting down at least an inch of water. Then stay off the overseeded area until well after the grass comes up—it will take two to four weeks.

SODDING A LAWN

Starting a lawn with sod is very satisfying. In one day, you go from bare soil to gorgeous green turf. It will cost you, though! Here are some times when it's worth the price to spring for sod:

● When you want or need an "instant lawn"

● When it's not the right time of year to sow seed

● When you need to start a lawn on a slope

Sod can come in rolls or stacked squares. Either way, you'll need to keep it moist until you're ready to lay it.

1. Find a Reliable Supplier

Before you buy sod, do some research about which grasses will grow best in your particular site. (Start by reading "Choosing the Right Grass" on page 17.)

Then search out a reputable nursery or sod farm that can provide you with a quality product. Sod should be fresh and re- cently harvested when it's delivered to your site and should, for best results, be laid within 24 hours of delivery. It should be thin (1 inch or less) for best rooting, but not so thin that it will be difficult to keep evenly moist.

2. Prepare the Soil

Make sure your soil is prepared before the sod arrives; see page 27. Allow the area to settle, and have the site completely ready by your delivery date. On planting day, rake the soil smooth and moisten it lightly.

3. Lay the First Row

Begin laying your sod against any straight edge, such as a sidewalk or driveway. To protect your prepared soil as you work, kneel on a board to distribute your weight over the soil.

4. Stagger the Seams

Lay the strips end to end, fitting the pieces together as tightly as you can without overlapping them. To prevent erosion channels from forming, stagger the seams in a pattern resembling the arrangement of bricks in a wall. If you're working on a slope, you may need to use wooden pegs or wire staples to hold the sod in place until the roots take hold.

It's easiest to get off on the right track by laying the first row of sod along a permanent straight edge.

5. Trim to Fit

Use a heavy-duty knife to trim the sod to fit around trees and the edges of structures and garden beds. After you've finished laying the sod, fill in any crevices with weed-free topsoil, and roll the sod with a light roller. Now turn on the sprinklers!

6. Care for Your New Sod

For the first two weeks, walk on your newly sodded lawn as little as possible, and keep it constantly moist. Try to water every day during the afternoon hours. Check for root development after 10 to 14 days by firmly grasping the grass blades and lifting vertically with both hands. When the sod resists, begin watering less frequently but more deeply (use more water each time) to encourage strong root growth. Continue this kind of tender loving care throughout your sod lawn's first growing season.

Stagger the edges of sod so you won't create a visible "seam" line where water can channel and erode the soil.

A heavy-duty knife comes in handy for trimming sod to fit around obstacles, as well as to trim the ends if needed to create a staggered pattern.

NEW LAWN CARE IN A NUTSHELL

After the time, trouble, and expense of putting in a new lawn, you want to take care of it properly so it grows up healthy, thick, and green. This handy reference will help you know what to do, and when, so you can get your new lawn off to a great start. For a more general lawn maintenance schedule, see the "Your Seasonal Lawn-Care Calendar" on page 96.

When to Plant

● If you're starting a lawn from seed, the best times to plant are spring and fall for cool-season grasses, and June and July for warm-season grasses.

● The best time to install sod is the same as for seeding; however, you can lay sod at other times if you're diligent about watering it.

When—And How Much—To Water

Like any plants you grow from seed, grass needs moisture to germinate. How much water may depend upon the type of grass you plant, but in general, here are some guidelines to follow:

After Seeding

● Water every day—even two or three times a day if it's very hot.

- Don't let the soil dry out completely, but don't flood the seeds, either.

- Water lightly, but regularly.

- Don't be impatient. It can take 7 to 35 days for grass seed to germinate, depending upon the species you've planted.

Once Grass Emerges

Don't stop watering! Continue to provide regular watering for 45 to 60 days after planting. Remember, these plants are just babies and they need time to get established.

When to Mow

- After about two or three months, your grass should be established enough to withstand being run over by you and your mower.

- Follow the mowing height guidelines for the type of grass you're growing. Most cool-season grasses should reach at least 3 inches before you mow them. Warm-season grasses, on the other hand, may need to be mowed at a shorter height.

- Don't mow off more than one-third of the grass height. Your grass is still young and you don't want to stress it any more than is necessary.

In General

- Keep off brand-new lawns. When grass plants first emerge, they're just thin spikes that can't take the abuse of people—or even pets—walking on them.

- Don't worry about weed seedlings. As your grass grows and thrives, it can crowd out any weeds that took the opportunity to grow in your freshly prepared soil.

PROBLEM-SPOT SEEDING

IF YOUR LAWN doesn't need a complete overhaul, you can repair problem areas by spot seeding. But before you sprinkle grass seed over the problem area, figure out *why* the problem occurred in the first place. Otherwise, that problem will probably return no matter how often you sow. Figure out the problem, fix it, and *then* rough up the surface and plant your grass seed! Here are some probable causes:

- A leaky hose connection causes water to puddle, encouraging weeds and diseases to take hold.

- A corner of the lawn is continually skipped when you fertilize.

- Gasoline from the mower was spilled (dig up ground; add 6 inches of organic matter).

- Heavy traffic from kids or pets causes wear (use a fence or pathway to divert traffic).

- Soil is heavy clay or too sandy (dig up ground; add 6 inches of organic matter).

It takes more than a lawn mower to keep your lawn in tip-top shape. Rakes and other hand tools are also important for maintaining your lawns.

chapter five

Tools of the Trade

When it comes to lawn-care tools, the number one item you need is a lawn mower. You'll also need some special equipment to use for trimming, raking, weeding, fertilizing, and watering your lawn.

10 ESSENTIAL LAWN-CARE TOOLS

Lawn mower. Power or push, this is one lawn tool you can't be without.

Trimmer. Trimmers let you cut grass in tight corners where lawn mowers won't fit. Handheld trimmers are powered by you (and don't pollute); power trimmers make quick work of bigger jobs.

Garden rake. A garden rake has a steel head that can be flat or bowed. You'll use it to prepare the soil before planting a lawn, and it's also practical for spreading compost over your lawn.

Leaf rake. If you—or your neighbors—have trees, you'll need a leaf rake to gather up piles of fall leaves.

Shovel or spade. Shovels are for turning the soil before planting or for doing spot repairs. Spades are great for making an edging between your lawn and garden beds and borders.

Garden fork. This tool lets you loosen compacted soil, and is handy for lifting and moving patches of sod or piles of compost.

Wheelbarrow. You won't want to be without this handy hauler, especially if you have a large lawn.

Sprinkler and hose. It's critical to water newly seeded or sodded lawns until they're established, so you'll need to have a hose. Likewise, a sprinkler is important for consistent, deep watering that you can't get from a hose and spray nozzle alone.

> **Power or push, a lawn mower is the one tool you can't be without.**

Spreader. Whether you choose a handheld model or a push type, this tool will help you spread fertilizer, compost, or grass seed.

Dandelion weeder. This little gadget helps dig out dandelions and other taproot weeds with ease. If you don't own one, you can use a trowel instead.

CHOOSING THE RIGHT MOWER

A lawn mower is the most expensive lawn-care tool you'll invest in. Prices can range from about one hundred to a couple of thousand dollars, so it pays to know what you want and what you need before you shop. Selecting the right lawn mower depends on the size of your lawn, its layout, your budget, and how much time you want to invest each time you mow.

A QUICK LOOK AT WALK-BEHIND MOWERS

Whether you shop at a lawn equipment dealer, garden center, home center, or even your local hardware store, you'll find mowers in all price and performance ranges. Here are some tips to help you narrow down your choices before you visit the stores.

Push mower. A typical push mower has a 3½- to 4-horsepower (HP) engine, 20- to 22-inch cutting width, and side-discharging deck. Push mowers are good for mowing flat lawns of one-half acre or less. Look for a model with extra-large rear wheels for easier turning.

Self-propelled mower. Engine power drives the front or rear wheels on self-propelled mowers, which have 4- to 5-HP engines. They're a

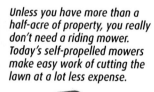

Unless you have more than a half-acre of property, you really don't need a riding mower. Today's self-propelled mowers make easy work of cutting the lawn at a lot less expense.

big help if you have a hilly lawn. Test-drive mowers before you buy to make sure the handlebars are easy on your hands.

Electric mower. Electric mowers start instantly and are much quieter than gas-powered mowers, but the cord limits their range to about 100 feet. Look for a model that has handlebars that flip over or that allow the cord to slide across the handle to reduce the chance of cutting the cord when turning the mower.

Battery-powered mower. Like electric mowers, battery-powered mowers are quieter than gas-powered mowers. While the range isn't limited by an electrical cord, your mowing time can be limited. Battery-powered mowers are convenient if your lawn can be mowed in less than 45 minutes; otherwise, the battery will need to be recharged before you finish the job.

Manual push mower. Also called reel mowers, newer manual models are lightweight and easy to push. Their self-sharpening blades neatly snip off the grass, instead of tearing it off like a power rotary mower. Reel mowers are quiet, nonpolluting, safe, and perfect for very small lawns.

Dedicated mulching mower. A mulching mower is a rotary mower with a closed, deep-domed deck that circulates the grass so it's cut several times by very sharp blades before being released back into the turf, where it decomposes rapidly. Look for mulching mowers with easily adjustable wheels so you can change the cutting height without fuss.

A dedicated mulching mower chops up grass clippings so fine that they decompose easily. There's no need to bag or rake them.

Multiuse mulcher/bagger. This is a rear-bagging mower that quickly converts from bagging clippings to mulching them, making it the best choice for home gardeners. You have the option of leaving finely chopped clippings on the lawn as fertilizer, or you can bag them and use them elsewhere as mulch or put them on your compost pile. Look for a mulching/bagging mower that has adjustable wheels so you can change the cutting height.

WALK-BEHIND MOWER TUNE-UP

TUNE UP YOUR mower (or have a professional do it for you) at least once a season. If you have a large lawn to mow, tune up your mower after every 25 hours of mowing. Here's a checklist:

- Change spark plug—cheap insurance that assures easy starts.
- Clean cooling fans to keep engine from overheating.
- Change engine oil, using the proper grade.
- Clean or replace the air filter to prevent stalling.
- Remove, sharpen, and balance the blade to prevent lawn damage.
- Clean the underside of the deck to increase cutting efficiency.
- Lubricate wheels and controls to prevent binding.
- Fill engine with fresh gas to assure good performance.

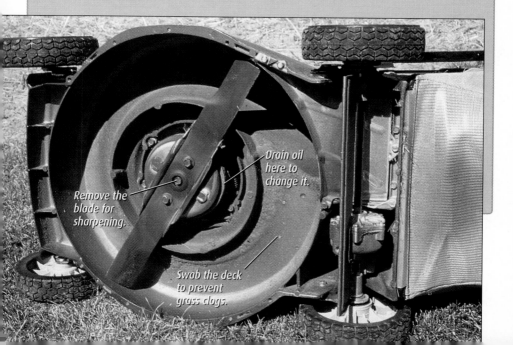

Drain oil here to change it.

Remove the blade for sharpening.

Swab the deck to prevent grass clogs.

THE BENEFITS OF REEL MOWERS

If you have less than a quarter-acre of turf to mow (or if you use a riding mower to cut a larger yard and need a smaller mower to do the trim work), you'll find that a reel or push mower can get the job done—and more. Don't be put off because they're old-fashioned. Because reel mowers use muscle power rather than gas, electric, or battery power, they offer real benefits. They don't pollute, they're quiet, they're lightweight and easy to use, they're better for your grass because they cut the blades cleanly like scissors would instead of tearing grass like rotary mowers do, and they don't blow exhaust in your face when you use them. One word of caution: While reel mowers cut cleanly, they can't handle tall grass or heavy-duty weeds.

Shopping Checklist

Here are some features to look for when you are shopping for a reel mower to make sure your mower will meet your needs and be easy to use.

Cutting width. The width can range from 16 to 20 inches. Wider widths let you cut the lawn in fewer passes, but a narrow width may be just what you need to mow grass paths between your flowerbeds or vegetable garden beds.

Cutting height. Make sure you'll be able to adjust the mowing height to at least 2½ to 3 inches. Some mowers have the highest height at about 1 inch, which isn't healthy for your grass.

Handles. Look for a model that has adjustable handles so you can mow with the handles set at a height that's comfortable for you.

Wheels. Check the tire tread (low-tread plastic models will slip more easily). Also, some types have a

quick tip

The extra effort you put into pushing your reel mower won't go unrewarded! A 150-pound person will burn about 400 to 450 calories in an hour of pushing a reel mower. That's enough calorie burn to help keep you fit and heart-healthy if you do it three or more times a week. Obviously, you won't need to mow your lawn three times a week, but you can take a day off from the treadmill or Stairmaster routine and get some delightful outdoor exercise this summer!

Don't let the simplicity of a reel mower fool you—this is one handy little cutting machine that can fit in places many other mowers can't.

RIDING MOWER TUNE-UP

JUST AS WITH a walk-behind mower, you need to have a riding mower tuned up at least once a season. If you have a lot of lawn to mow, tune up your mower after every 25 hours of mowing. Here's a checklist:

- Check electrolyte level/ battery charge for quick starts.

- Check electrical system for loose connections to avoid stalls.

- Lubricate all linkages for smooth operating.

- Change engine oil and replace air filter for long engine life.

- Change spark plug for good fuel economy.

- For a clean cut, check mower deck for blade sharpness.

- For an even cut, check tires for proper inflation.

- Check all safety devices and debris guards—a must!

double set of wheels while others have a roller bar on the back. Double wheels are better because they don't flatten the grass like the roller models can.

Blades. When the blades are tuned to cut properly, they actually sharpen themselves as they cut.

Weight. Reel mowers can weigh from about 20 to 40 pounds. If you have a lot of hills on your property, how much mower you have to push uphill is an important consideration!

Riding Mowers

Highly maneuverable and simple to operate, a riding mower is actually a multipurpose garden tool. While it can be a major investment, if you have the jobs, it can do the work. It mows the lawn and it's also a tow vehicle; just hitch it up to a cart and you'll be able to easily move large loads of soil, sod, or your garden's harvest. Add a bagging attachment to quickly collect all the shredded leaves or grass clippings you need for mulching or to add to your compost pile.

Riding mowers make quick work of a lawn because of their wide cutting width. Choose a model with a tight turning radius and you'll be able to get in tighter spots and have less trimming work to do.

EDGERS AND TRIMMERS

While mowing will take care of cutting most of your grass, you may have areas where your mower can't get close enough to mow. Installing mowing strips around beds (see page 95) and planting beds along the edges of fences are ways to cut back on the amount of trimming you'll have to do. But you'll probably still have some grass trimming to tend to.

Hand trimmer. A hand trimmer may not be glamorous, but it gets the job done. If you don't have a large property with lots of trimming to do, choose either trimmers that look like sheep shears or a scissors type. Both operate by squeezing the handles together.

Hand trimmer

String trimmer. Power trimmers have a replaceable nylon string that whirls at high speed to cut grass, weeds, and anything else in its path.

String trimmer

Turf edger. With a semicircular metal blade attached to the end of a long handle, a turf edger is designed to do exactly what it says. It lets you cut through turfgrass to make nice neat edges—especially along sidewalks and driveways. Each time you use a turf edger, you cut off a little bit of soil, so don't use it more than once a year to neaten your lawn.

Turf edger

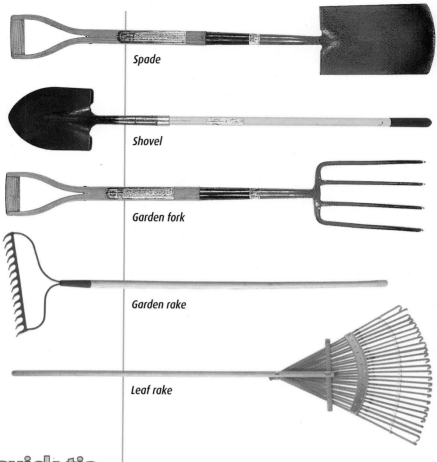

Spade

Shovel

Garden fork

Garden rake

Leaf rake

quick tip

Try tools out before you buy them. Make sure they're not too heavy for you to handle or too lightweight for your needs. The handle length should be comfortable for you to use, too. If you're taller than average, look for longer-handled tools, often sold with names like "Backsaver."

SHOVELS, RAKES, AND FORKS

A shovel with a rounded-point tip is good for hauling and digging. Spades generally have rectangular shapes, and the edge is sharp for digging into sod to create new beds or edge existing beds. In either case, look for a solid rather than open back—it's stronger.

A steel garden rake as well as a lawn rake (available in steel, polypropylene, and bamboo) are important to own, too. Lawn rakes come with wide and narrow fan-shaped heads—a wide one lets you sweep up more grass at a time, but choose one that's easy to maneuver.

If you grow zoyziagrass (which requires de-thatching), consider investing in a thatching rake, which has multiple blades to cut through the thatch.

A garden fork has four tines that are 10 to 12 inches long. It's great for loosening heavy clay soil, as well as for turning and spreading compost.

HAND TOOLS

A trowel is a great garden tool, but when it comes to lawn work, the only reason you'd need one is for digging out weeds. So look for a narrow-bladed trowel, preferably with a one-piece steel blade, rather than one that is riveted. You can get by without a trowel for weeding if you have another type of weeder in your toolshed.

A pronged dandelion weeder is great to help with the task of uprooting unwanted dandelions or other taproot weeds. Use its long handle as a lever to dig deep under the soil and pry up pernicious weeds.

Trowel

SPRINKLERS

If you're starting a new lawn, you'll need to water the seed or sod until they're established. Watering manually with a hose won't let you get the job done right. You'll simply lose patience standing there holding the nozzle long before you've done an adequate, deep watering. So invest in a sprinkler to help you water effectively.

Dandelion weeder

Types of Sprinklers

Revolving sprinklers. These operate by shooting water out of two or three arms that are spun around by water pressure. They're inexpensive, but they don't cover much ground, and the coverage isn't uniform.

Fixed sprinklers. Fixed sprinklers shoot water through a pattern of holes in the sprinkler head. Many have a dial that you can turn to select a sprinkling

BUYING A GOOD HOSE

YOU'LL NEED A HOSE to use with that sprinkler. Here are some hose buying and care tips:

- Hoses prices vary according to how many plies of material they have (the more plies, the more durable the hose).

- Rubber hoses are generally more durable than nylon and vinyl hoses.

- Look for a hose with solid brass couplings.

- Buy a ⅝- or ¾-inch diameter hose; ½- and ⅜-inch hoses are too small for lawn-care tasks.

- Hang your hose properly—on a hose hanger or reel, not on a nail! And hang it so it won't be exposed to excessive sunlight.

- Don't let your hose kink—it leads to cracking.

- Always drain your hose before rolling or hanging it up.

- Store it in a dry place over the winter—not outside.

pattern: circle, square, fan, semicircle, and so on. Fixed sprinklers tend to be the leakiest and cover the least amount of ground.

Oscillating sprinklers. Coverage is in a rectangular pattern as a central perforated tube rocks back and forth and sprays water. Many can be adjusted to water only to one side. Be sure to buy a quality model that doesn't puddle water at the farthest reach of its throw.

Impulse sprinklers. These operate by shooting water out in a jet, which is broken into small drops by an adjustable diffuser pin. The force of the water also turns the sprinkler head. These sprinklers cover the greatest range and do so pretty uniformly; however, water can accumulate near the base of the sprinkler.

Traveling sprinklers. The arms are like those of a revolving sprinkler, but the base travels along the lawn, dragging the hose behind it. A traveling sprinkler provides even coverage, but at a low precipitation rate. You may have to let it travel over your lawn a few times to water deeply.

An impulse sprinkler (left) shoots a powerful spray, but you can adjust its force with the built-in diffuser. An oscillating sprinkler (right) can also be regulated—to move back and forth, or to simply spray in one direction.

SPREADERS

Spreaders are useful for spreading grass seed, applying fertilizers (organic, of course!) and compost. Choose from handheld models (good for small areas) or push spreaders, which hold more.

Broadcast spreaders. Material is dropped from the hopper onto a pan that rotates, flinging seed or fertilizer by centrifugal force. Broadcast spreaders cover a large area quickly, but the coverage isn't uniform—you'll get less material at the farthest edges than in the center.

Drop spreaders. Seed or fertilizer drops through holes in the bottom of the spreader, so it falls evenly across the area—which is only as wide as the spreader itself. It takes longer to cover an area with a drop spreader than a broadcast type, but the coverage is more uniform. Make two passes with a drop spreader; after covering the lawn in one direction, cover the area again, working perpendicularly to your first pass.

A broadcast spreader has a rotating pan below the hopper that distributes the seed. It's effective for spreading seed over a large, flat area. For hilly terrain, a drop spreader works best.

WHEEL-BARROWS

YOU MAY NOT NEED a wheelbarrow on a weekly basis, but it will make taking care of your lawn much easier. A wheelbarrow is handy for hauling compost, topsoil, mulch, leaves, bags of grass seed—or whatever you need to get from one side of your property (or your car's trunk) to another.

Wheelbarrows are easier to maneuver than heavy-duty lawn carts because they have one wheel, not two. If you have a quarter-acre of ground or less, a light-duty steel wheelbarrow may be sufficient for your lawn needs. However, if you buy the biggest wheelbarrow you can afford, you can move big loads in fewer trips.

So if a large contractor's wheelbarrow fits your budget, buy it. It can carry a heavier load, but works equally well on small jobs. It has a larger wheel to support heavy loads, and if you buy a plastic model with wooden handles, maintenance is minimal—no metal parts to rust.

Fertilizing, watering, mowing—it doesn't have to be a vicious cycle. Follow our low-maintenance techniques, and you'll actually have time on the weekends to sit back and relax!

chapter six

Lawn Maintenance Made Easy

Of course you want a beautiful lawn—but you also *don't* want to spend hours looking after your lawn. That's the beauty of organic lawn care: It doesn't require tons of time and effort to keep your lawn looking good, and you won't have to spend a bundle of money, either.

In this chapter you'll learn the organic way to feed and water your lawn to cut down on weeds and other problems. You'll also discover that you don't have to mow your lawn the same way week in and week out, just because it's Saturday. Follow the mowing, watering, and fertilizing guidelines in this chapter, and your lawn will be on its way to being healthier and lower maintenance than ever before.

THE ART OF MOWING

Mowing is the most important part of lawn maintenance. That's because mowing can be the most beneficial thing you do for your lawn—or the most harmful. How and when you mow has a big effect on the health and appearance of your lawn—its vigor, disease resistance, and weediness. Mowing also affects your lawn's need for water and fertilizer. Proper mowing can kill weeds, cure disease, save water, and provide fertilizer. And the keys to proper mowing are mowing at the right height and leaving the clippings on the lawn.

If you're an average American homeowner, you spend 40 hours a year behind a lawn mower. Chances are, your mowing technique fits one of two styles: You mow every week, at the same time and in the same

How and when you mow has a big effect on the health and appearance of your lawn.

JUST BECAUSE you want to go organic with your lawn maintenance doesn't mean you have to do all the work yourself. If you prefer to hire a service to mow and trim your lawn as well as to fertilize it as needed, just be sure to specify to the company what you want.

There are many landscaping companies that use chemicals, but there are those that don't. Some lawn-care services provide both chemical and organic-based services. While you're checking, don't forget to specify your preferred mowing height, too.

way; or you wait until your backyard begins to look like a meadow before you finally give in and mow. Both of these approaches leave a lot to be desired if you want a healthy and attractive lawn. Instead of mowing when it suits *your* schedule, your goal should be to mow your grass when it's the proper height— which may be less than weekly at some times of year, and only once every few weeks at other times.

Vary your cutting patterns every time you mow to assure even growth and to avoid compacting the soil under your lawn. If you mow parallel to the street one week, mow perpendicular to it the next time you mow.

LEAVE GRASS TALL

The simplest way to help your organic lawn grow up healthy and thick is to adjust your mower's cutting height to its highest setting. Why? Tall blades of grass have more surface area exposed to the sun, so they can photosynthesize more easily and produce more sugars and starches to help fuel root growth. Grass with a large root mass is better at taking up water and nutrients, so plants are more tolerant of drought and can recover more rapidly from dormancy. Tall grass also outcompetes annual weeds and conserves moisture by shading the soil.

Aim for 4 Inches Tall

For most grasses, the ideal mowing height (the shortest you should cut your lawn) is 3½ to 4 inches. Some varieties, particularly fine fescues and centipedegrass (see pages 21 and 23 respectively), fall over at that height and should be mowed shorter than other grasses.

Leave the Clippings

As grass clippings decompose, they contribute valuable nitrogen to the soil—almost 2 pounds of nitrogen per 1,000 square feet of soil each season. They also add organic matter and provide many other benefits to the soil and grass. (For details, see "Leave the Clippings Where They Fall" on page 54.) Many people believe, however, that clippings left on the lawn contribute to thatch—dead or dying grass parts that form a layer on top of the soil and prevent moisture and oxygen from reaching plant roots. But just the opposite is true: Fresh clippings stimulate earthworm activity, which breaks down thatch.

Keep the Blade Sharp

A dull lawn-mower blade will tear grass, making a jagged wound on each individual blade. Disease organisms can infect these wounds, and the grass will lose water rapidly through evaporation from the open wounds. To save your grass from pain, sharpen the mower blade after every eight hours or so of cutting. (Most hardware stores and any power-equipment dealer will sharpen your blade quickly and inexpensively.)

Letting your grass grow longer isn't only better for the grass, it's much more comfortable to relax on, too!

quick tip

Mow no more than one-third of the grass blade's height to avoid stressing the grass and to encourage a deeper root system. So if you mow when your grass reaches 4½ inches tall, you should remove about 1½ inches *at most* when you mow.

LEAVE THE CLIPPINGS WHERE THEY FALL

LETTING THE CLIPPINGS fall back onto the lawn when you mow is a lot less work than bagging them, and it's better for your lawn, too! When researchers at the University of Connecticut compared two cool-season lawns—one with the clippings removed and the other with the clippings left behind—they found that the latter was healthier because it had:

- 45 percent less crabgrass

- Up to 66 percent less disease

- Up to 45 percent more earthworms

- 60 percent more water reaching the grass roots

- 25 percent greater root mass, which means less room for weeds and more drought tolerance for grass

- 50 percent reduced need for nitrogen fertilizer

Sometimes It's OK to Remove Clippings

There are four instances when it can be a good idea to rake up your grass clippings.

1. When converting from a chemically treated lawn to organic methods—especially if you already have a thatch problem. When you first switch, rake up the clippings because the soil under your lawn probably doesn't contain enough earthworms to process the clippings. Once your lawn is pesticide-free for a season, you should have enough earthworms to do the job.

2. After the first spring mowing. Removing the clippings will help your grass green up.

3. After the last fall mowing. Removing clippings then can help reduce the chance of disease.

4. Whenever you cut off more than one-half of the top growth of your grass. Especially if you don't use a mulching mower, the clippings can be large and take longer to decompose.

When you do rake or bag your clippings as you mow, don't throw them into the trash. They make great mulch (as long as they weren't chemically treated) or can add a quick boost of nitrogen to your compost pile.

FEEDING YOUR LAWN

Every lawn needs to eat. But knowing when to fertilize and how much fertilizer to apply depends on more than just how green (or brown!) your lawn looks. If you live in an area of the country where your lawn goes dormant during part of the year—either in the heat of summer or in the cold of winter—it's understandable that you're anxious for it to turn green again. Instead of using color as a cue for feeding your lawn, the following schedule will help you decide when and how much fertilizer to use.

When raking up clippings, don't bother with bagging them in plastic. Simply rake them onto a tarp, then drag them to your compost pile or garden. You won't have to keep bending to pick up the clippings.

The Best Time to Fertilize

Your fertilizing schedule will depend on where you live and the type of grass you're growing. The following guidelines are based on growing low-maintenance lawns in the five grass-growing zones in the United States. (See "What's Your Region?" on page 18 for more on your region's zone.) The "Grasses' Nitrogen Needs" chart on page 56 shows how many pounds of nitrogen make up a full dose for the type of grass you're growing.

ZONE 1: THE HUMID NORTHEAST. Provide a full dose in fall after the grass stops actively growing.

ZONE 2: THE HUMID SOUTH. For summer grasses, provide one-half dose in June and one-half dose in August. For winter grasses, provide a full dose in September or October.

quick tip

While grass clippings can be good for your lawn, a thick cover of fallen leaves shouldn't be left on the lawn all winter. They mat down and smother the grass below. If you don't have a chipper/shredder, you can use your lawn mower to shred the leaves. Just rake the leaves into a pile and run your mower over them in a crisscross pattern until they're cut into small pieces. Then toss them on your compost pile.

ZONE 3: THE GREAT PLAINS. Provide a full dose in September.

ZONE 4: THE DRY SOUTHWEST.

For summer grasses: Provide a full dose in October or November and again in May or June for cool-season species with irrigation; provide one-half dose every month from May to August for warm-season species with irrigation; and provide one-half dose in April or May and one-half dose in August for warm-season species without irrigation.

For winter grasses: Provide a full dose in October or November.

ZONE 5: THE HUMID NORTHWEST. Provide a full dose in October or November, or after grass stops ac-tively growing.

Nitrogen Needs

While grass needs a variety of nutrients, nitrogen is the number-one need, and the chart below shows you just how much nitrogen the type of grass you're growing requires. Check out the "Natural Nitrogen Numbers" chart on page 58 to see what kind of food you can use to provide the proper amount of nitrogen to your lawn.

GRASSES' NITROGEN NEEDS

Pounds of nitrogen per 1,000 square feet/year

Species	Pounds Needed
Bahiagrass	2
Bermudagrass	1
Kentucky bluegrass	2
Buffalograss	1
Centipedegrass	2
Fescue	1
Perennial ryegrass	2
St. Augustinegrass	2
Zoysiagrass	2

Choosing the Right Fertilizer

Natural organic fertilizers such as bloodmeal are the best type to apply on lawns because they are slow-acting. They include slow-release nitrogen, phosphorus, and potassium. They'll help your lawn grow and stay healthy, but the lawn won't grow so fast that it's impossible to keep up with all the mowing.

Organic Options

Organic fertilizers are, for the most part, moderate in nitrogen content, neutral in pH, and water-insoluble—just what the lawn ordered. They're lower in nitrogen than synthetic fertilizers and may be more expensive, pound for pound, in the short run. But because they're kind to your lawn, and you don't have to apply them nearly as frequently, organic fertilizers can actually save you money. In addition, organic fertilizers don't harm organisms beneficial to the soil, such as earthworms. As a result, you have more worms and organisms helping to break down thatch, which helps prevent pest and disease problems. (For more on this, see "The Truth about Thatch" on page 60.)

You can buy all types of organic fertilizers—from chicken manure to alfalfa meal—at most lawn and garden centers.

There are plenty of natural sources for nitrogen, and most are available at garden centers. Dried poultry manure, for example, is a good value—one 40- or 50-pound bag will feed 1,000 square feet of lawn per year. The following table lists your options along with application rates.

TO GREEN UP a lawn that's suffering from heat stress, spray liquid seaweed on the grass, following the label directions for lawns. It may take several applications (again, refer to the package for specifics), and you must keep the lawn watered once it greens up again.

Use a hose-end sprayer to spray the seaweed solution, and apply a double dose along the edges of the lawn that border sidewalks and your driveway where reflected heat increases the stress on the grass.

Instead of using liquid seaweed, purchase seaweed powder and mix it with water at home to make your own concentrate. Not only can you mix small amounts as needed, you'll also save up to 30 percent of the cost of preformulated seaweed solutions.

NATURAL NITROGEN NUMBERS

Pounds of organic fertilizer needed to provide 1 pound of nitrogen per 1,000 square feet of lawn

FERTILIZER	POUNDS
Alfalfa meal	10
Bloodmeal	10
Cottonseed meal	15
Dried poultry manure	25

Applying Fertilizer

Whichever type of fertilizer you use, you can apply it with the same spreader you use to spread grass seed. For more information on selecting and using a spreader, see "Spreaders" on page 49.

WATER WISELY

When it comes to your lawn, the best way to save time, money, and precious water is to stop pampering the grass. Lawn grass can survive some pretty tough conditions, as long as it has deep roots. If you help your lawn develop those deep roots, it will be prepared for dry weather and you may never have to water it. How can you encourage your lawn to grow deep roots? Water *infrequently*: That way your grass will have to send roots farther down in the soil to find moisture.

Northern lawns seldom die of thirst, even if they aren't watered at all, provided they're planted in good soil with plenty of organic matter and are mowed properly. Northern grasses handle the heat and dryness of summer by going semidormant. The grass may be brown for a few weeks, but don't worry: It will snap back as summer draws to a close and temperatures become more moderate.

Southern lawns, on the other hand, may require that you keep watering during the hot summer weather. Bermudagrass is able to go a long time without water, but it must have some. St. Augustinegrass is shallow-rooted and must be watered often. Many California lawns are Kentucky bluegrass, and they must be watered weekly in summer.

Deciding When to Water

You may have read or heard that you should give your lawn 1 inch of water each week, but it's just not so. The 1-inch-per-week is a generalization, but not all lawns need the same amount of water, and not all soils hold the same amount of water.

So rather than watering on a schedule, watch your grass for signs that it truly needs water. If your lawn turns dry and brown during its normal growing season (spring and fall for cool-season grass, summer for warm-season grass), that's a sign that you need to water it.

When you do water, your method of watering should depend on the type of soil you have. If your lawn is growing in heavy clay soil that can hold lots of water, it makes sense to water deep and long. But sandy soils drain too quickly to benefit from a long watering session. Instead, you'll need to water for a shorter period, and water a few times in succession to help your lawn recover.

Remember, water your lawn only during the growing season. If cool-season grass is less than green during the height of summer, that's natural—watering won't help make it greener. Depending on where you live, you may be able to go for years without ever watering your lawn: Mother Nature will supply all that's needed.

A sprinkler is handy when establishing a new lawn, but other than that, you probably won't need to water on a regular basis unless your lawn starts looking brown during its season of active growth.

Thatch certainly indicates that you have a problem, but it's not caused by grass clippings. Thatch is an overabundance of grass stems and roots, which is caused by chemical lawn treatments that kill off earthworms, soil compaction, and over-watering—all things you can fix.

THE TRUTH ABOUT THATCH

Here are three common myths about thatch:

1. All thatch is bad.

2. Grass clippings are the main component of thatch.

3. Raking up grass clippings helps prevent thatch.

Myth 1 Debunked

The latest research on lawns shows that a little thatch isn't bad at all. It may even do some good. Thatch returns nitrogen to a lawn, and when it's less than ½ inch deep, it can act as mulch for your lawn.

If your thatch layer is deeper than ½ inch, you could be asking for trouble. A thick thatch layer can prevent water from penetrating to the soil and serves as a breeding ground for insects. It also harbors diseases, especially brown patch and dollar spot.

Myth 2 Debunked

Grass clippings typically start breaking down and releasing nitrogen to the soil within a week, so it doesn't hang around long enough to be part of thatch. Thatch is made up mainly of roots, creeping stems called stolons, and underground stems called rhizomes.

Myth 3 Debunked

Naturally, since grass clippings aren't part of thatch, raking them up won't help prevent thatch. One of the best ways to prevent thatch is to avoid using any chemicals on your lawn. Treating your lawn with chemicals can kill or repel the earthworms and microorganisms that help in the decomposition of roots and stems. Overwatering, soil compaction, and improper mowing can also add to a thatch problem.

Preventing Thatch

In a healthy lawn, earthworms pull thatch underground, eat it, and turn out humus. If you've got a good supply of earthworms in your soil, you won't have thatch.

If you're switching from chemical to organic lawn care, however, you may have an earthworm shortage, and thatch can build up. To encourage these natural thatch-busters in your soil, give them what they want—turf that's free of chemicals and fertilizers, moderate amounts of natural nitrogen, and lots of organic matter. How do you supply all that? Topdressing.

Topdressing for Thatch

Topdressing is simply adding a layer of organic material on top of your lawn to improve the soil base without digging up the lawn and starting over.

Rx for thatch: Spreading a layer of finely screened compost on top of your lawn is one of the easiest things you can do to help build better soil, encourage earthworms, and in general, boost the health of your lawn.

BEST CHOICES FOR DROUGHT TOLERANCE

SOME GRASSES handle drought better than others. Here's a rundown of the major grasses and their drought tolerance.

Drought-Tolerant

Bermudagrass

Zoysiagrass

Buffalograss

Tall fescue

Fine fescue

Moderately Tolerant

Kentucky bluegrass

Perennial ryegrass

St. Augustinegrass

Bahiagrass

Drought-Susceptible

Creeping, velvet, and
colonial bentgrasses

Annual bluegrass

Centipedegrass

Annual ryegrass

Topdressing reduces thatch by speeding up the natural decomposition process. Finely screened compost, which you can have delivered from a nursery or make yourself, is one of the best topdressings you can use. It takes about ¾ cubic yard of compost or topsoil to cover 1,000 square feet of lawn. Give the entire lawn a layer no thicker than ⅜ inch, using a fertilizer spreader, in the fall.

DETHATCHING—IS IT NECESSARY?

Unless you have a serious thatch problem, adding compost or topsoil annually will help keep the situation in check; dethatching isn't needed. For moderate thatch, a good stiff raking with a thatch rake (see "Shovels, Rakes, and Forks" on page 46) will do a thorough job of removing it. But if thatch has formed because your soil is worn-out and compacted, then your problems are more serious. You can remove the thatch, but it will be back unless you improve the soil. In this type of extreme case, you may need to aerate the soil—literally poke it full of holes—to get better air circulation and the life back into your soil.

A specially made thatch rake, which can be found at most garden centers, slices through thick layers of thatch to loosen the soil and let water and air reach grass roots.

The Lowdown on Aeration

If you decide to aerate your lawn, you have several options, depending on how hard you're willing to work and how much money you're willing to spend.

Pitchfork. A simple way to aerate the soil yourself is to use a pitchfork to poke holes in the soil. If you have a big lawn, this will take you quite a while, but it's fairly easy to do. Push the pitchfork 4 to 6 inches deep into the lawn, then rock it back and forth slightly.

Pull it out and repeat at equidistant intervals until you've covered the whole lawn.

Core cultivator. This inexpensive tool has a handlebar at the top and two or four hollow tines at the base. Step on the tool to poke holes in the soil and then lift the handlebar to pull up cores of soil and thatch. As you press the tool into the next section of turf, the cores will be pushed out of the tines and onto the top of the turf. Once you've finished cultivating, you can break up the cores using a rake. You'll aerate and top-dress your lawn at the same time!

Aeration sandals. One-size-fits-all spiked sandals let you aerate a lawn simply by walking on it.

Power walk-behind aeration machine. You can rent a machine or hire someone to do the job for you. This tool can make quick work of aerating, without damaging the turf or requiring that you dig up the sod and start over.

A simple pitchfork or garden fork (left) is one tool you can use to loosen compacted soil. Just press the fork into the ground, wiggle it, and repeat in the next spot.

Aeration sandals (right) slip on over your work boots. When you walk on your lawn, the spikes aerate it. It will take some time to cover a large lawn, but it does work!

It may look like a weed to you, but to a child, a dandelion seedhead is a puffball of fun. When you're dealing with weeds and other lawn problems, remember that you don't need to wipe out every last weed and pest to have an attractive lawn.

chapter seven

What to Do about Weeds, Diseases & Pests

Keeping weeds, diseases, and pests from troubling your lawn is up to you, not your grass. If you mow, water, and fertilize your lawn correctly, chances are you'll have few problems with nasty weeds and pesky pests. But occasionally, something in your lawn may get out of whack, and you'll need to take action to restore your lawn to health. Read on to find out the best organic ways to fight weeds, diseases, and pests.

WHAT TO DO ABOUT WEEDS

When it comes to lawns, "weedy" is in the eye of the beholder. Sure, lawns are made of turfgrass, but what's wrong if your lawn has some flowering plants in it, too? It's up to you to decide what you call a weed, how many weeds you can stand, and which ones absolutely have to go.

If you want your lawn to look like a putting green, then everything but bentgrass is a weed. But if the purpose of your lawn is to serve as a pretty place to play ball with the kids or have a barbecue, then you can stretch the definition of what's acceptable.

There are two cases when you should take action against weeds or risk losing your lawn: when more than 25 percent of your lawn is dominated by a single type of weed, or when you have less than 25 percent turfgrass in your lawn overall.

When you decide to fight weeds, don't try to get rid of all of them at once. Pick the one that annoys you the most, and go after that one first.

> **When you decide to fight weeds, don't try to get rid of all of them at once. Pick the one that annoys you the most, and go after that one first.**

JUST A FEW DECADES AGO, A CLOVER LAWN WAS A SIGN OF PRESTIGE. CLOVER'S SILKY GREEN LEAVES AND PASTEL FLOWERS MAKE DELIGHTFUL LAWNS THAT ARE SOFT TO WALK ON AND PRETTY TO LOOK AT. CLOVER ALSO MOWS WELL AND SMOTHERS OTHER SO-CALLED WEEDS. UNTIL THE 1950S, CLOVER WAS AS COMMON IN HOME LAWN MIXES AS BLUEGRASS IS TODAY. IT'S AMAZING THAT MODERN HOMEOWNERS SPEND TIME AND MONEY STRUGGLING TO GET A BEAUTIFUL PLANT LIKE CLOVER OUT OF THEIR LAWNS.

Why Some Weeds Are Good

You may find it hard to believe, but having a few weeds here and there in your lawn is actually good for it. Lawn weeds can attract and provide shelter for beneficial insects (those that eat the pesky insects that damage plants). Weeds can help protect your lawn from disease attacks, too. Because many diseases attack particular species, having more than one species of grass in the lawn ensures that your entire lawn won't succumb to a single disease. And some weeds offer other benefits: For example, dandelions are edible and white clover provides nutrients to the soil.

What about Dandelions?

Are they really weeds? Not to the kid making dandelion chains or blowing puffballs. Not to the wine enthusiast who brews dandelion wine. And not to the farmers who raise dandelions to sell as a cash crop. (The tasty greens are harvested and sold in farmer's markets and sent to supermarkets.) So ask yourself if you can stand a few dandelions in the lawn. What harm are they doing? They're not likely to ruin a picnic!

CORN CUTS WEEDS

YES, THERE IS A SAFE, organic substance that kills lawn weeds. Corn gluten meal, a nontoxic by-product of corn processing, prevents seedlings from growing new roots and kills them within a few days. Not only that, it contains 10 percent nitrogen, so it's a fertilizer, too. Best of all, kids and pets can play on the lawn right after you apply it.

Researchers at Iowa State University found that applying corn gluten meal one time—before weeds emerged—reduced the survival rates of dandelions, crabgrass, annual bluegrass, buckhorn plantain, curly dock, purslane, lamb's-quarters, and redroot pigweed by an average of 60 percent. After several years, corn gluten meal provides as much as 90 percent control.

Remember to use corn gluten meal only on established lawns—it will kill newly sprouted turfgrass. Also keep in mind that if you use it, you should cut back on the amount of any other nitrogen fertilizer you use on your lawn.

8 WILD LAWN WEEDS

-- CRABGRASS ----------------------------------

Crabgrass (Digitaria spp.) *emerges in late spring— especially after a rainy spell— and hangs around all summer, growing faster than turfgrasses.*

Description: A warm-season annual with thick, hard stems that spread along the ground and straight up

Favorite sites: Lawns where the grass has been cut too short, allowing sunlight to reach crabgrasses' low-growing stems

Quick fix: Dig out the plants completely—new crabgrass can grow from any remaining roots—and sow grass seed where the weed grew. Or, spread corn gluten meal on your lawn in spring *before* overwintering seeds germinate. (See the opposite page.)

Long-term prevention: Mow your lawn on the high side of the recommended height range. Manually remove weeds from reseeded spots until the lawn grass can compete with the weeds.

Reason to live with it: Crabgrass stays green during droughts—a time when most turfgrasses turn brown.

-- BROADLEAF PLANTAIN ----------------------

Broadleaf plantain competes for space wherever turfgrass has a tough time growing.

Description: The wide, egg-shaped leaves of broadleaf plantain (*Plantago major*) form a ground-hugging rosette. It's a perennial; the leaves sprout up in midspring and by early summer a long seed-covered stalk emerges.

Favorite sites: Dense, compacted soil, as well as moist shaded sites and high-traffic areas

Quick fix: Use a pronged dandelion weeder to lift the rosette and pull the long taproot from the soil.

Long-term prevention: Apply compost to improve soil structure. Loosen compacted soil by aerating it. In shade or high-traffic areas, plant turfgrass that will tolerate those conditions. (See "Choosing the Right Grass" on page 17 for recommendations.)

Reason to live with it: A poultice of crushed plantain leaves relieves the itch caused by poison ivy.

Dandelions are prolific self-sowers, but you can enjoy them while they punctuate your lawn in yellow. Simply mow or pick them before they set seed.

Description: In early spring, dandelions (*Taraxacum officinale*) sprout narrow, serrated leaves from a thick, strong taproot. After the yellow flower fades, a white puffball of seeds forms; they blow away to sow new plants.

Favorite sites: Dandelions grow in almost any conditions, quickly colonizing thin spots in your lawn.

Quick fix: Use a V-shaped dandelion weeder to dig out tops and taproots completely. If you don't get all of the root, try again when the plant resprouts. For large patches, spread corn gluten meal in early spring before seeds sprout (see page 66).

Long-term prevention: Encourage a dense stand of turfgrass. Remove dandelions *before* they form seedheads.

Reasons to live with it: Young dandelion leaves taste great in early spring salads.

It's easy to understand why ground ivy is also called creeping Charlie, as its long stems grow quickly, covering a lot of ground in a hurry.

GROUND IVY

Description: A bright green perennial vine, ground ivy (*Glechoma hederacea*) quickly forms a mat of stems that take root wherever they meet the soil. Small purple-blue flowers appear in late spring and continue through early summer.

Favorite sites: Ground ivy thrives in the shade, where many turfgrasses do not.

Quick fix: Rake it out—this weed has very shallow roots and comes out with a simple tug. Put the pulled ivy in direct sunlight or in a hot compost pile where it will quickly shrivel and die.

Long-term prevention: In deep shade, instead of trying to grow turfgrass, plant a nongrass shade-loving groundcover such as pachysandra or sweet woodruff (*Galium odoratum*).

Reason to live with it: It's not a weed—it's a shade-loving groundcover!

-- CHICKWEED --

Description: Chickweed (*Stellaria media*) features long, spindly stems with small oval leaves spread to form a low-growing mat in cool months. As the weather warms, the plant quickly shoots upward and bears small white flowers that produce thousands of seeds.

Favorite sites: It thrives in sunny, moist areas, especially where turfgrass dies out during the winter because it's not hardy enough. Chickweed also takes hold easily in lawns that are mowed too short.

Quick fix: Use a cultivator to pull out the weed and its shallow roots *before* it flowers and scatters its seeds.

Long-term prevention: Plant turfgrass that can survive your winter conditions, such as tall fescue in the North or zoysiagrass in the South. Mow the lawn on the high side.

Reason to live with it: You can eat it raw or cooked; it tastes a bit like spinach.

Chickweed is an annual that sprouts in the fall, survives over the winter, flowers the following spring, and then dies.

-- ANNUAL BLUEGRASS ------------------------------------

Description: The leaves of annual bluegrass (*Poa annua*) are lighter green and rougher in texture than those of Kentucky bluegrass (*P. pratensis*), its perennial cousin. Annual bluegrass turns "dead" brown in dry summers.

Favorite sites: It loves damp, compacted soil and often shows up in overfertilized Kentucky bluegrass lawns.

Quick fix: Pull, hoe, or till small bunches. Corn gluten meal also is effective against annual bluegrass.

Long-term prevention: Apply compost and aerate to improve soil drainage. Feed your lawn only with slow-release organic fertilizers and stick to the low end of your turfgrass's nitrogen recommendations.

Reason to live with it: In spring, it looks enough like turfgrass to make your lawn seem thick and green.

Annual bluegrass starts out looking great in spring, but when it turns dead brown in dry, hot summers, you'll be wishing you had perennial bluegrass growing in its place.

Perennial quackgrass spreads rapidly and is tough to get rid of. When you dig out the rhizomes, resow the area densely with turfgrass seed to prevent its return.

QUACKGRASS

Description: Quackgrass *(Agropyron repens)* has long, narrow leaves and fibrous stems that emerge in early spring. It spreads by seed and, more aggressively, by a dense network of underground stems.

Favorite sites: It thrives in the same conditions as turfgrass—full sun, moist soil, moderate fertility.

Quick fix: Use a hand weeder and your fingers to extract the weed's shallow but extensive root system. Every bit of quackgrass left behind can grow into a new stand.

Long-term prevention: Use straw, not hay (which can contain weed seeds), as mulch where you're trying to establish turfgrass. If you already have a quackgrass problem, don't till the area—it will only spread the problem.

Reason to live with it: Dried quackgrass deters slugs.

You can learn to appreciate the dots of white clover flowers in your grass or fertilize your lawn with nitrogen—a nutrient that's sure to be missing where clover is growing.

WHITE CLOVER

Description: White clover *(Trifolium repens)* has stems of three-part (four if you're lucky), dark green leaves that grow 2 to 3 inches tall and white globe-shaped flowers that bloom on thin stalks. Clover grows in masses in sunny sites, starting in late spring. Flowers appear through midsummer.

Favorite sites: Clover moves into spots where turfgrass is sparse and the soil is low in nitrogen.

Quick fix: Till to remove clover, then mix compost into the soil to increase its water-holding capacity and fertility. Reseed bare spots with grass.

Long-term prevention: Feed your lawn a slow-release, nitrogen-rich organic lawn fertilizer in early spring and fall for a cool-season grass, or in mid- to late spring for a warm-season grass.

Reasons to live with it: Pretty clover flowers attract pollinating bees to your garden.

CAN THIS LAWN BE SAVED?

WHEN IT COMES to getting rid of clover, the first question you should ask yourself is, "Can I live with it?" Clover is pretty, and it adds dots of white highlights scattered through an otherwise endless sea of green grass. Plus, it adds nitrogen back into the soil.

On the other hand, since clover moves in where grass is thin or spotty, its presence may also mean you have a more severe problem that is preventing grass from growing. So before you take any radical steps to get rid of clover (or any other "weed" for that matter), do a soil test.

From compaction to low fertility to poor drainage, weeds can be your first clue that something is wrong with the soil. ("Start with the Soil" on page 9 explains ways to improve problem conditions.) Whether you decide to live with the clover or improve your soil to make it easier to grow turfgrass, look at the clover (or whatever weeds you're growing) as an indicator of what's wrong with your soil. It's a great place to start to find the right fix.

4 DREADED LAWN DISEASES

When lawn diseases strike, don't reach for the chemicals! There are plenty of other ways to fight lawn disease. All you may need to do is change the way you're mowing or watering your lawn, and the problem may disappear. Diseases can also be a problem if your soil pH isn't right, and adding lime may make your lawn healthy again.

Choosing resistant grass varieties can help prevent diseases in the first place. But when you do notice a lawn disease, rest assured that most are relatively easy to handle. On the following pages, you'll find descriptions and photographs of some of the most common lawn diseases, along with what causes them—and how to help your lawn recover.

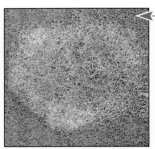

Brown patch, the most widespread lawn disease in the United States, shows up in hot, humid weather.

BROWN PATCH

What it is: Brown patch causes circular patches—from a few inches to several feet in diameter—to appear in the lawn. The patches look dark and water-soaked at first, and eventually the grass dies and turns brown.

Susceptible grasses: All species of lawn grass

What causes it: Close cutting, poor drainage, over-watering, excessive nitrogen, and a low pH level all contribute to brown patch.

How to get rid of it: Control brown patch by cutting back on nitrogen fertilizers, mowing less frequently, and top-dressing with organic matter. Water less frequently and only during the day so grass dries quickly. Rake out dead grass and replant bare spots with grasses resistant to brown patch.

Dollar spot starts out as spots the size of silver dollars (thus the name) and develops into spreading blotches if left unchecked.

DOLLAR SPOT

Description: Patches of grass with round, bleached spots with brown edges. Each spot is about the size of a silver dollar.

Susceptible grasses: Bluegrass, bahiagrass, bermudagrass, centipedegrass, bentgrass, Italian ryegrass, fescues, St. Augustinegrass, and zoysiagrass

What causes it: Dollar spot is most likely to strike in summer when the soil is dry and low in nitrogen. The warm days and cool nights of early and late summer are apt to encourage it.

How to get rid of it: High mowing can control the disease once it strikes. Cutting off the tips of the grass removes the infected area, slows the disease's spread, and helps the grass recover quickly. When your lawn is suffering from dollar spot, make frequent, light applications of high nitrogen fertilizer. A well-fed lawn is less susceptible. Overseed in the fall with resistant varieties of grass.

RED THREAD

Description: Lawns infected by red thread fungi will have circular patches of dried grass that have red or rust-colored threads on the blades.

Susceptible grasses: Bermudagrass, bentgrasses, Kentucky bluegrass, ryegrass, and fescues

What causes it: Red thread is a fungus that occurs during the cool, wet weather of spring and fall in the Northeast and Pacific Northwest. It also occurs as a winter disease of bermudagrass in the South.

How to get rid of it: To control the fungus, apply an organic fertilizer with nitrogen in a readily available form such as a seaweed foliar spray. Regular mowing removes infected leaf tips and lessens the severity of the disease. Lawns that are watered deeply on a regular basis tend to be less susceptible.

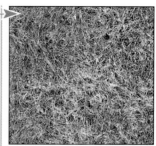

The red tips of grass infected with red thread (or the related pink thread) disease are more conspicuous when grass is wet.

FAIRY RINGS

Description: This disease appears in the spring as circles of dark green grass. A ring of grass around the dark green spots turns brown, and eventually the green areas will brown out, too. After a rain, mushrooms may appear on the circumference of the ring. Eventually the mushrooms parasitize the grass roots, causing them to die.

Susceptible grasses: Bluegrass, fescue, and bentgrass

What causes it: This fungus occurs in areas of high rainfall such as the Pacific Northwest.

How to get rid of it: Fairy rings is among the most difficult of lawn diseases to eradicate. The only sure way to get rid of the mushrooms is to dig them out and turn the soil to a depth of 2 feet, extending outward at least 1 foot beyond the edge of the circle. You can slow the fungus by saturating the soil with water to a depth of 2 feet. Otherwise, you may be simply have to live with the disease.

Fairy rings may sound charming or even mystical, but the ring of toadstools is really caused by a fungus that grows in damp weather conditions.

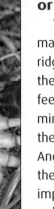

quick tip

Always investigate a pest problem before you reach for the pesticide—even if it is organic. Until you know which pest is troubling your grass, you won't know what method of control is appropriate to use.

GRUBS, BUGS, AND A RODENT OR TWO

You may never see some of the pest insects that live in and around your lawn, and that's okay. While there probably are a few pests in the grass, you don't need to worry about them unless you see strong signs of their damage. If you're managing your lawn organically, chances are that your lawn also hosts plenty of beneficial insects that eat pests—there's a natural balance between the pests and the predator insects, and you don't need to intervene.

You also may never spot the animal pests that most commonly bother lawns: moles, voles, and skunks. That's because they either spend most of their time underground or are active mainly at night. While their tunneling and digging may be annoying, these animals won't do too much damage to your lawn, and there are some simple things you can do to reduce their damage.

Moles often get a bad rap when it comes to lawns. But they're actually beneficial because they eat grubs, which are true pests that can kill your grass.

Moles—Friend or Foe?

Yes, moles do sometimes make annoying mounds and ridges in your lawn, but they're also beneficial, feeding on grubs and stirring mineral-rich subsoil up into the root zone of your grass. And mole tunneling aerates the soil, which in turn can improve plant growth and reduce soil erosion.

Moles live almost entirely underground, so you're unlikely to ever see them. What you will see are the unique aboveground ridges they make as they tunnel through the soil searching for food. Unlike other underground critters such as gophers and voles, moles don't eat your precious plants' roots. Instead, they're looking for a meal of fat, white grubs like those of Japanese beetles.

What to do about moles: Sometimes roots are disturbed by moles digging, but you can minimize any permanent damage to your lawn by pressing mole ridges flat and watering the area well. If mounds cause problems when you mow, raise the mower's cutting height. You can also shovel some of the dirt off the mound and sprinkle it over the tunnels you pressed down.

Vole Damage

If you have tunnels in your yard and you're finding dying plants or bulbs that fail to come up, you probably have a *vole* problem. Voles really aren't a lawn problem—they're micelike critters that feed on the roots of many garden plants, not lawn grasses. So don't blame voles for digging tunnels in your lawn—they simply use *mole* tunnels to avoid predators. If you do see a vole popping out of a tunnel, you'll know you've also got moles around the yard.

What to do about voles: You can trap voles with mousetraps baited with peanut butter or apples. Set the traps near the vole hole, and put a box over the hole to encourage the voles to emerge from the hole.

Scavenging Skunks

Skunks can cause minor damage by digging in your lawn, but instead of worrying about the skunk, take care of the real problem—grubs. Like moles, skunks like to feed on grubs.

What to do about skunks: If you catch a skunk digging in your lawn, refer to the "Common Lawn Pests and Remedies" chart on page 76 for ridding your lawn of the grubs. It's a lot safer to treat grubs with milky disease spore than it is to chase down a skunk!

ENDOPHYTE GRASSES FIGHT PESTS

IF YOU HAVE a bug-plagued lawn, you can overseed it with special types of grasses called endophyte-containing cultivars. Endophytes are fungi that produce a substance that naturally repels some pests and is toxic to others that feed on grass crowns and lower stems. So with an endophytic grass, you'll have fewer worries about chinch bugs, sod webworms, billbugs, and armyworms. (Sorry, grubs can feed on endophytic grasses without ill effect). *Note:* The toxin is harmful to sheep, cattle, and pregnant mares, so don't seed endophyte-containing grasses in grazing areas.

Overseed shady lawns with insect-resistant fescue. You can also use fescue in full sun areas, or use insect-resistant perennial ryegrass varieties. Look for named varieties in grass seed mixtures sold in garden centers or mail-order catalogs. Since these grasses have less than a two-year shelf life, buy only the freshest seed.

Common Lawn Pests and Remedies

Even when you plant pest-resistant grasses and maintain your lawn well, some insect pests may occasionally pose a threat. Here's a chart of the most common insect pests and what to do about them.

SYMPTOM	CULPRIT	REMEDY
Bare or ragged patches	**Armyworms** are pale green caterpillars about 1½ inches long that eventually turn greenish brown with white side stripes before changing into gray-brown moths. They chew grass blades down to the crown. They are common pests on bermudagrass during cool, wet periods.	Spray affected areas with parasitic nematodes while armyworms are present. Spray in late afternoon or evening, too, so the nematodes won't dry out. Spraying with BTK also works. (See "Quick Tip" on the opposite page.) Remove dead areas of turf. Reseed with resistant grasses.
Yellowed grass; thinned, brown turf	**Bermudagrass mites** are microscopic white mites that suck sap from grass blades, causing them to turn yellow or straw-colored. They thrive on poorly fed lawns during dry conditions.	The best controls are to improve fertility and keep the lawn well watered during dry spells.
Yellow circular patches	**Billbugs** are cream to brown or almost black, ¼- to ½-inch weevils. Their white grub larvae feed on grass stems, causing shoots to turn brown and die. In warm weather, the grubs tunnel into the soil and feed on roots and stolons (underground stems).	Control billbug grub problems by aerating the lawn, watering deeply in spring to encourage deep root growth, and removing thatch (if your lawn has a thatch buildup). Reseed or overseed with resistant cultivars.
Yellow circular patches	**Chinch bugs** have small black bodies with a black triangular pad between white, folded wings. They are serious lawn pests throughout the country, especially in dry conditions. The adults suck plant sap; infested grass turns yellow, and patches may die off. The nymphs, tiny bright red insects with a white band across their backs, also suck sap and cause the most damage. These pests usually congregate in open, sunny parts of the lawn.	In moist soil, a naturally occurring fungus keeps chinch bugs under control, so if you have a chinch bug problem, control it by keeping the soil very moist. Wet soil to a depth of 6 inches, and maintain that moist condition for 3 to 4 weeks.

SYMPTOM	CULPRIT	REMEDY
Chewed grass	**Grasshoppers** chew on grass but are not often a serious threat to an entire lawn.	The protozoan *Nosema locustae* kills grasshoppers, but the effects aren't usually realized until the second summer after application. Broadcast the bait (see "Recommended Reading & Resources" on page 100) as soon as grasshoppers emerge in the spring.
Irregular streaks of brown grass through lawn	**Mole crickets** are 1½-inch-long light brown insects with short forelegs and shovel-like feet. They are serious lawn pests in the South, tunneling under the lawn and feeding on grass roots.	Parasitic nematodes are an effective control. Water the soil well before and after application. Apply during late afternoon or evening to avoid the drying effects of the sun.
Irregular, brown, dead patches	**White grubs** are the curved, fat larvae of Japanese and other beetle species. They chew on grass roots, leaving sections of lawn that appear burned and can be easily lifted from the ground. Ten or more grubs per square foot is a serious infestation. Grubs are most common on cool-season grasses.	Apply milky disease spores. This bacteria survives for years in the soil and will eliminate Japanese beetle grubs over the course of a few seasons. Apply the material in late spring or fall when soil temperature is at least 70°F, but while grubs are still present.
Small, dead spots	**Sod webworms** sever grass blades just above the thatch line and pull the blades into a silken tunnel in the ground to eat. As they feed and tunnel, irregular, dead patches appear. Sod webworms are a problem on bluegrass, hybrid bermudagrass, and bentgrasses in the South. Hot, dry conditions and thatch buildup encourage the pests.	Control webworms by saturating infested areas with a soap drench (2 tablespoons of liquid detergent to 1 gallon of water) to float the larvae to the surface. Rake the pests into a pile and dump them into a bucket of soapy water. Use insecticidal soap to ensure the pests are killed. Applying BTK when pests are in their larval stage (usually about two weeks after moths appear) is an effective control.

quick tip

BT, or *Bacillus thuringiensis,* belongs to a group of bacteria that isn't toxic to humans and other mammals, but when eaten by certain insects (mainly caterpillars), it kills them. Apply BT, or a variety called BTK, as a spray, following directions and taking care to not to let the spray drift to uninfected or weedy areas where the caterpillars you want to protect (butterfly larvae) may be feeding.

Every family needs some lawn area for play, but you'll find your yard is a more enjoyable place to be when the grass shares the spotlight with trees, shrubs, and colorful flowers.

chapter eight

Beyond the Traditional Lawn

Nothing beats a lawn for playing catch, and a smooth, green swath of lawn sets off flowerbeds perfectly. But too much lawn can be boring to look at and time-consuming to mow. Why not convert some of that grass into a beautiful bed of groundcovers or an island of colorful flowers?

THE BEST USE FOR YOUR BACKYARD

How much lawn you really need depends on how you use your yard: Parties and picnics? Ball playing and swing sets? Sunbathing and strolling? Once you decide, you can determine exactly how much of the high-maintenance green stuff you need, and how much space you can devote to other, less labor-intensive landscape options. Here's a sampling of your choices:

- Low-maintenance groundcovers with attractive foliage or flowers
- Aromatic herb lawns that are pretty and useful
- Beautiful butterfly garden or meadow
- Tree and shrub borders or island beds for shade and beauty

When it comes to care-free plantings on tough-to-mow sites, groundcovers are the answer.

GET TO KNOW GOOD GROUNDCOVERS

Many groundcovers, such as moss pink (*Phlox subulata*) and mother-of-thyme (*Thymus serpyllum*), tolerate mowing and foot traffic. Flowering groundcovers, such as spotted lamium (*Lamium maculatum*), will add color to your landscape, and berry-bearing groundcovers, such as wintergreen (*Gaultheria procumbens*), will attract wildlife.

When it comes to care-free plantings on tough-to-mow sites, groundcovers are the answer. Review this handy checklist *before* you buy:

- Match plant choices to your site conditions—sun, shade, water, soil type, heat and cold, and foot traffic, and ask at the nursery for those that have a proven track record in your area.

- Mowing tolerance is important if you'll routinely be mowing around the groundcover area.

- Plants that spread by runners or stolons (underground stems) will fill an area more quickly than clump-forming plants.

- Evergreen groundcovers look good year-round and offer protection from soil erosion.

- When it comes to appearance, choose groundcovers based on leaf texture and color. Flowers are merely a short-term bonus.

- Plants with dense growth habits discourage weeds.

7 REASONS TO GET RID OF SOME LAWN

1. To conserve water
2. To stop mowing
3. To attract beneficial insects so you won't need pesticides
4. To attract butterflies
5. To feed and provide habitat for birds and other wildlife
6. To use your yard to restore native plants
7. To increase your home's energy efficiency

GETTING READY FOR GROUNDCOVERS

Beautiful, thick, weed-smothering areas of ground-cover start with thorough soil preparation, especially in difficult sites. Preparing the soil helps get your groundcovers growing quickly and gives them a head start over weeds.

You'll need to remove the sod, then prepare the soil, tilling deeply and adding organic amendments. For specifics on preparing your area, see "Preparing the Site" on page 27.

TACKLE TOUGH SITES WITH TERRIFIC GROUNDCOVERS

Dry, shady sites, such as the areas under shade trees and shrubs, beneath eaves, and on shaded slopes, are some of the toughest challenges a gardener faces. Constantly wet areas are trouble spots, too. And sunny slopes are awkward to mow. Before you despair of ever having anything grow in these areas, try a groundcover that's partial to those conditions.

5 Great Groundcovers for Dry Shade

Lawn grasses have a hard time growing in shade, especially dry shade. Instead of struggling to maintain a lawn under these conditions, replace it with ground-covers that will thrive.

- **Ajuga** (*Ajuga reptans*): Green, purple, or variegated leaves with blue, white, or pink flowers; 4 to 6 inches tall. Zones 4 to 8.

- **Epimediums** (*Epimeduim* spp.): Evergreen or semi-evergreen, heart-shaped foliage; 6 to 12 inches tall. Zones 3 to 8.

- **Wintercreeper** (*Euonymus fortunei*): Glossy ever-green leaves; 4 to 6 inches tall; will climb trees. Zones 4 to 8.

quick tip

Since it takes most ground-covers two years to fill in, apply mulch at planting time and replenish it as needed to keep weeds out. Check the area often during the first two years and re-move weeds when they're young and easy to pull.

Periwinkle or vinca will fill in an area in just one season and provide year-round green, even when the pretty lavender-blue flowers aren't in bloom.

- **Lilyturfs** (*Liriope* spp.): Green, grasslike foliage with purple or white flower spikes; 18 inches tall. Zones 5 to 9.

- **Common periwinkle** (*Vinca minor*): Trailing, evergreen plant with shiny, dark green foliage and lavender-blue or white flowers; 4 to 6 inches tall. Zones 4 to 9.

4 Groundcovers for Soggy Sites

Even if you get grass to grow in a soggy area, the spot is usually too wet to mow. Instead, fill in the moist spots with groundcovers that enjoy the dampness. The plants below will thrive in moist to wet soil in sun or shade.

- **Lady's-mantle** (*Alchemilla mollis*): Pale, gray-green foliage that is velvety soft to the touch with sprays of yellow-green flowers; 12 inches tall. Zones 3 to 8.

- **Astilbes** (*Astilbe* spp.): Fernlike foliage with white, pink, or red flowers; 1 to 4 feet tall, depending on species. Zones 3 to 8.

- **Hostas** (*Hosta* spp.): Bold and beautiful heart-shaped or lancelike leaves in many sizes and shades of green; many variegated types, with white or lavender flowers in summer; 6 to 48 inches tall, depending on species. Zones 3 to 8.

The cool yellow green of lady's-mantle will brighten up a shady spot but looks just as lovely in sunny locations, provided there is sufficient mositure.

- **Creeping Jenny** (*Lysimachia nummularia*): Small rounded leaves with yellow flowers; 2 to 4 inches tall. Zones 3 to 8.

5 Sunny-Slope Contenders

If pushing and pulling a lawn mower up slopes isn't your idea of fun, put a stop to steep-site maintenance with fast-growing plants and a cover of mulch to conserve moisture.

Summer-blooming maiden pinks add a touch of old-fashioned charm and a delightful fragrance wherever you plant them.

- **Maiden pinks** (*Dianthus deltoides*): Narrow, blue-green leaves; pink or white flowers; 6 to 12 inches tall. Zones 3 to 9.

- **Wintercreeper** (*Euonymous fortunei*): Trailing or climbing evergreen plant; many types with variegated leaves; 1 to 2 feet tall. Zones 4 to 9.

Perennial candytuft is a low-maintenance contender for hot, sunny slopes. Because it's evergreen, it provides year-long coverage in addition to a welcome burst of pure white flowers in spring.

- **Perennial candytuft** (*Iberis sempervirens*): Dark, evergreen leaves; flat, bright white flower clusters in spring; 6 to 12 inches high. Zones 3 to 9.

- **Junipers** (*Juniperus* spp.): Needle-leaved evergreen available in many forms, from prostrate, 6-inch-tall types to large trees. Select a variety that matures to a height that's best for your site. Zones 3 to 9, depending on species.

- **Thymes** (*Thymus* spp.): Creeping, fragrant-leafed herbs with tiny white or pink flowers; foliage may be variegated; 1 to 12 inches tall. Zones 5 to 9.

5 Tough Plants for Shady Slopes

If you have a shady slope, replace the hard-to-mow grass with one of these easy-care, shade lovers.

- **Ajuga** (*Ajuga reptans*): Green, purple, or variegated leaves with blue, white, or pink flowers; 4 to 6 inches tall. Zones 4 to 8.

- **Epimediums** (*Epimedium* spp.): Spreading plant with evergreen or semievergreen leaves; small yellow, pink, bronze, or white flowers in early spring; 5 to 12 inches tall. Zones 3 to 8.

- **English ivy** (*Hedera helix*): Evergreen vine; 6 to 8 inches high when creeping on the ground; will climb trees to 50 feet. Zones 5 to 9.

- **Japanese pachysandra** (*Pachysandra terminalis*): Glossy green leaves; plant spreads by runners; white flowers; 6 to 9 inches tall. Zones 5 to 9.

- **Common periwinkle** (*Vinca minor*): Trailing evergreen plant with shiny, dark green leaves and lavender-blue or white flowers; 4 to 6 inches tall. Zones 4 to 9.

A hillside of English ivy complements the brighter green of the grass it borders, and it's much lower maintenance. An occasional pruning around the edges is all it takes to keep this bed in shape.

CALCULATE YOUR COVERAGE

WHEN PLANTING GROUNDCOVERS, you can choose just one or use a combination. If you use a mixture, it's best to group each type separately rather than mixing them together. In general, space plants 6 to 10 inches apart (measuring from their centers) in staggered rows.

To get quicker and more uniform coverage, buy plants in 4-inch or bigger pots, and pull apart the individual plantlets in each pot. Plant the pieces a little more closely, and the sections will fill in the spaces quickly.

To determine how many plants you'll need, multiply the number of square feet of the area to be covered by the number of plants you plan to use per square foot. For instance, if you want to use 3 plants per square foot and the groundcover garden area is 6 feet square, you'll need 18 plants.

SWEETLY SCENTED HERB LAWNS

While many people think grass is a must in high-traffic areas, there are other plants that work just as well under fairly heavy foot traffic. Low-growing herbs such as dainty-but-tough thymes and free-ranging mints can make excellent groundcovers. And herbs offer bonuses that grass lacks. Tread on them or nick them with trimmers, and they'll perfume the air for you. Many herbs are also perfect when you're in a pinch for something to season tonight's dinner! Here are some great-smelling choices:

Roman chamomile (*Chamamelum nobile*): Forms a soft, dense carpet of fine yellow-green foliage that resembles Irish moss.

- Unlike Irish moss, chamomile is sturdy enough to be walked on.
- Undisturbed, chamomile can reach 9 inches tall, but light foot traffic keeps it low enough to make mowing unnecessary.
- It's a fast spreader—individual plants that are planted 6 inches apart will fill in solidly in a single season.
- The yellow-centered flowers that rise above the mat add an attractive touch.
- It's not a good choice if you're allergic to ragweed, as Roman chamomile and ragweed are related.

Sweet woodruff (*Galium odoratum*): A shade lover with a light, sweet fragrance that registers differently with different people—some smell vanilla, others new-mown hay.

- Sweet woodruff is well suited as a groundcover under trees.
- It grows rapidly and covers quickly, continuing to spread by self-seeding once established.
- Its tiny white flowers look delicate, but sweet woodruff is hardy to at least 30°F (Zone 4).

quick tip

Some trees are nearly impossible to grow grass under because they have many surface roots that compete with grass for root space, water, and nutrients. Avoid planting the following trees in prime lawn areas: Norway maple, silver maple, birches, beeches, and elms.

Here a bed of thyme is kept in check by deep edging between it and the lawn.

ROSEMARY— FOR THE WARM CLIMES

IN CALIFORNIA, rosemary (*Rosmarinus* spp.) is often used as a groundcover in city flowerbeds, but the standard type is a bit rangy. A creeping form with an interesting, random growth habit, however, can make for a very good groundcover.

Prostrate rosemary is strictly no-traffic when it's young, but after it matures, the woody stems can take some stepping with no lasting damage.

Rosemary isn't bothered by reflected heat such as that radiated by sunny walls or sidewalks. So use it as an accent along a patio or terrace or at the base of a stone retaining wall for a stunning effect. Unfortunately for folks living in the cooler climates, this groundcover is only hardy in USDA Zone 8 and south.

This lawn of thyme has a more natural look because it's not contained as a border or edging.

Mints (*Mentha* spp.): Legendary for their invasiveness, but if it's a lawn you want, mints make a tough, dense groundcover.

- Weeds don't stand a chance of competing when up against established mint.
- Grow mint where it can spread at will without causing harm or where it can be easily confined.
- Hardiness varies with variety from subtropical all the way up to Zone 3.
- Corsican mint (*M. requieni*) is tiny and too tender to walk on, but it makes a very tight, low-growing mat only 1 inch or so high that looks great between stepping stones, or as a filler in beds.
- Pennyroyal (*M. pulegium*) makes a good groundcover—either by itself or planted into an existing lawn. It's tough enough for light traffic and is easy to keep low by mowing.

● Peppermint (*M.* × *piperitum*) mixes nicely with grass. Mowing keeps it low, and the grass helps cushion it from heavy foot traffic. Don't use it to replace grass; it's a complement that has a wonderful scent that makes mowing more pleasant.

Thyme (*Thymus* spp.): Not just for the kitchen anymore. Creeping woolly thyme is a good groundcover choice, but other creeping varieties are also available.

● Creeping varieties grow low and spread quickly.

● Thymes sport colors ranging from light lemon yellow to deep grayish green.

● Originally native to dry regions, most thymes grow well in dry, poor soil, and they actually *require* such hardships to develop their best flavor.

● Many thymes are hardy down to -30° to -40°F.

quick tip

Explore the area under your trees with a hand trowel before you plant groundcovers. Find open areas between established tree roots, then dig small holes or "pockets" for plants.

EROSION MATS MAKE PLANTING SLOPES EASY

SPREADING GROUNDCOVERS will eliminate your mowing and weeding chores fast if you anchor plants with fabric mats for a quick start. They hold soil and new roots in place and block weeds at the same time. Inexpensive mats made of burlap or paper are available at garden centers; avoid landscape fabric because it won't biodegrade.

Roll the burlap or mats out and secure them to the slope with wire pins. (You can make your own wire pins by cutting V-shaped sections from wire clothes hangers.) Arrange plants on top of the mat, then lift each plant and cut an X through the mat with a sharp knife to make a hole large enough for the rootball. Fold the edges back, dig a hole, and plant. Then fold the edges back around the plant. Mulch over the mat when you're finished planting to disguise it and to conserve moisture.

SET THE STAGE for success by choosing the right kind of meadow plants.

- **Choose a regional mix.** Most seed companies and nurseries offer both wildflower and grass-and-wildflower mixes that are designed for specific parts of the country.

- **Avoid "instant meadow" mixes.** They are mostly annual flowers or inexpensive generic wildflowers.

- **Save on weeding with aggressive wildflowers.** A mix of vigorous wildflowers won't give you the variety a more carefully planned and developed meadow will provide, but it will get you a flower-filled meadow fast. Try perennials like common yarrow, Queen-Anne's-lace, dame's rocket, oxeye daisy, and evening primrose. In two to three years, they'll take over and choke out any other plants with very little help from you.

ENJOY THE BEAUTY OF A WILDFLOWER MEADOW

Creating a meadow, as more and more people are discovering, is a way to make part of your lawn area more inviting to birds, butterflies, and other wildlife. Each part of the country has native wildflowers that are favorites of the birds of that region. Wherever you live, a wildflower meadow will provide food and cover for all sorts of birds and butterflies, such as goldfinches, hummingbirds, indigo buntings, and monarch butterflies.

Start Small

If you're considering planting a meadow garden, the best advice is to start small. Removing sod to prepare the site for a new planting involves a bit of work, so you won't want to dig up your entire yard at once. Select a section of your backyard where you'll have the opportunity to observe the planting through all the seasons before you make over your entire lawn.

Think Big

Keep in mind that a meadow looks distinctly different from a closely cropped lawn. Whether you choose groundcovers or a mix of native grasses and wildflowers, the look will be more tufted and will change through the seasons. Some native prairie or meadow plants can even grow as tall as 4 to 8 feet!

What you decide to plant is based on what you want and where you live. For example, if you live in the Midwest, you could install a prairie planting. But if you're in the Southwest, the environment is too dry and hot for those plants; a more appropriate choice would be desert groundcovers or a blend of native grasses and groundcovers.

Don't skimp when it comes to selecting plants and buying seed. Your meadow will be a thing of beauty

Meadows work just as well on sloping terrain as they do in flat spaces. Here the care-free look of a small meadow planting provides pretty counterpoint to the rigid structure of a deck.

for years to come, so you won't want to waste time or money on plants that won't thrive. If your budget is tight, increase the percentage of grasses. They're a little less costly than some of the native prairie flowers. Besides, grasses form the backbone of the meadow.

6 Steps to a Great Meadow

1. **Prepare the soil.** First you'll need to remove the grass or whatever is growing in the area where you want a meadow. Mow the grass low, and then turn under any remaining vegetation with a rotary tiller, which can be rough going, or rent a sod cutter to remove the sod completely. Then till the soil and add organic amendments. See "Preparing the Site" on page 27.

2. Plant. The best time to plant in Zone 3 and warmer is about one month before the first killing frost in fall. In colder zones, plant as soon as the soil can be worked in spring.

Broadcast the seed, walk on it to press it into the soil, and cover with straw to keep the soil from drying out. As an alternative, you can set transplants in the soil, rather than starting from seed.

3. Water. Keep seedlings or transplants moist until they're established—about four to six weeks.

4. Mulch. When the seedlings are large enough to identify as flowers and not weeds, apply 3 to 4 inches of organic mulch.

5. Weed. Walk through the meadow occasionally during the first year and pull out unwanted plants.

6. Mow. Starting the year after planting, your meadow will need to be mowed once a year in early spring. Use a string trimmer or scythe and cut 4 to 6 inches above the ground so you won't disturb the plant crowns. You can hire someone with the proper equipment to mow large meadow areas.

LIVEN UP GRASSY AREAS WITH COLORFUL BULBS

Spring bulbs are often our first sign of spring—they can sprout even before the first robins show up! But bulbs aren't just for flowerbeds. They look great naturalized in grassy areas, too. Each spring they can give your lawn a colorful meadow look, then when mowing begins, you'll never know they were there.

Small bulbs are best for naturalizing—they're easier to plant and they bloom reliably year after year. You can even plant them under deciduous trees, because they'll be up and blooming before the trees leaf out and create their summer shade. Here are some to try:

Crocuses speckle the lawn in full color in very early spring. By the time you're ready for the first lawn mowing, their blooms are gone.

- Grecian windflower (*Aneomone blanda*)
- Crocuses (*Crocus* spp.)
- Common snowdrops (*Glanthus nivalis*)
- Summer snowflake (*Leucojum aestivum*)
- Grape hyacinth (*Muscari armeniacum*)
- Daffodils (*Narcissus* hybrids)
- Siberian squill (*Scilla sibirica*)

To create a carpet of springtime bloom in an existing lawn, simply make a hole in the grass with a narrow trowel, dandelion digger, or garden knife. For small bulbs, you can just wiggle your tool back and forth to create a small hole and slip the bulb in place. For larger bulbs, you may have to actually lift the sod and soil, insert the bulb, and put the flap of turf back in place.

If you have a lot of large bulbs to place, use a spade or shovel and remove larger areas of turf—about 1 foot square. Loosen the soil, plant the bulbs, replace the turf, and water.

quick tip

To get a good show of blooms in the first year of bloom, plant the bulbs in clumps, rather than spacing them apart as individuals. Plant daffodils 6 inches deep, but other bulbs only 3 or 4 inches deep.

CREATING ISLANDS OF BEAUTY

Another way to cut back on lawn care while increasing the value and enjoyment you get from your landscape is to start with existing features, like a tree or shrub in your lawn, or a fence along the edge of your lawn, and create a garden around the feature.

Dealing with Tree Roots

Instead of struggling to grow and mow grass under trees, plant shade-tolerant shrubs and groundcovers under trees, then mulch for a low-maintenance planting you'll enjoy for years to come. If you have shallow-rooted trees such as maples and beeches, there will be lots of fibrous roots to work around. Deep-rooted trees such as oaks have more root-free places to plant. Whichever type of tree you have, take care not to damage large roots, and don't remove more than 5 percent of smaller roots while planting.

Mowing strips installed around landscape plantings make trimming around beds a snap—just run your mower along the strip and forget about sessions with a string trimmer.

Add just enough compost to fill your holes and bring new plants up to the original soil level. Never bury the crown of a tree or it will decline; oaks and sugar maples are particularly vulnerable.

When All Else Fails, Mulch

Some shady areas defy gardening attempts, and that's when mulch makes the easiest groundcover of all. A layer of bark mulch can give you a care-free, weed-free surface instantly; it's especially good for unsociable sites like under black walnut trees or the heavy shade of southern magnolias. Spread mulch all the way out to the drip line for easier mowing, no weeding, and happy trees.

Mowing Strips Ease Maintenance

Use edging strips around island beds to keep lawn grass from overtaking your islands. You can mow around them with a single pass and won't have to trim by hand. To install a brick mowing strip, use a sharp spade to dig a brick-size trench around your bed. Starting at one end of the trench, lay the bricks in side-to-side, butting them snugly against each other and leveling them as you go. Backfill as necessary and sweep dry soil into the spaces between the bricks.

GOT A FENCE? ELIMINATE THE HASSLES

Plantings of trees, shrubs, groundcovers, and easy-care perennials can eliminate tedious weeding or trimming along a fence. Select plants suited to the site, then plant and mulch. No more snagging the mower on the fence or coming back later with a trimmer.

If you need to be able to paint your fence occasionally or need access to plants from the back, leave a 2-foot-wide, mulched maintenance path between the fence and the plants.

FUN FACT

IF ANIMAL PESTS SUCH AS DEER, SQUIRREL, OR MICE HAVE EATEN EVERY BULB YOU'VE EVER PLANTED IN YOUR BACKYARD, THERE'S STILL A BULB YOU SHOULD TRY PLANTING. WHILE MOST BULBS ARE AS APPEALING TO ANIMALS AS POTATO CHIPS ARE TO HUMANS (THEY CAN'T EAT JUST ONE!), YOU'LL BE HAPPY TO KNOW THAT DAFFODIL BULBS ARE POISONOUS TO ANIMALS. BUT DON'T WORRY ABOUT HARMING THE ANIMALS. THEY HAVE ENOUGH SENSE TO STAY AWAY FROM THESE NATURALLY DANGEROUS BULBS.

Your Seasonal Lawn-Care Calendar

JANUARY

Check out the **reel mowers** in your local hardware store. (If the store doesn't carry them, tell somebody in charge that they should!) Winter's also a great time to think about how you use your yard and **plan a project** to convert some lawn to another use such as a meadow, island bed, or outdoor entertaining area.

Add **lime** or **sulfur** to correct pH, if recommended by soil test (see "August" on the opposite page). Also, winter is a great time to think about how you use your yard. Why not plan a project to convert some lawn to another use?

FEBRUARY

Sharpen your mower blades, or take them to a nearby shop to have them sharpened. Now's a good time for a **mower tune-up**, too—you can beat the crowds. A properly working mower will generate less pollution. While you're at it, set your **mowing height** at 3 inches or higher.

If you have a power mower, take it in for a **tune-up** ahead of the spring crowds. **Sharpen** your mower blades, and consider buying a **spare blade** so you'll always have sharp blades on hand.

MARCH

Clean up any debris left on the lawn after the winter.

Your **first mowing** should be in early spring. The **mowing height** depends on the type of grass you're growing. Refer to "Choosing the Right Grass" on page 17 for specifics.

APRIL

As the grass begins to grow, you can begin to **mow**—but don't remove more than one-third of the height of the grass blades at each mowing. You might want to bag or rake up the **clippings** after the first mowing to **add** a good dose of **nitrogen** to your compost pile. But after that, leave the clippings on the lawn!

Warm-season grasses are actively growing now, so **water as necessary** during this season of growth, and keep on mowing.

MAY

Spread organic fertilizer. There's not much point in doing this before midmonth, as it won't begin to act until the soil warms. Water as necessary during the grass's active growing season. Deep watering, enough to wet 6 inches down into the soil, encourages healthy roots. Mow weekly or even every five days if your grass is growing rapidly.

In addition to mowing, **spread organic fertilizer**. Different grasses have different **nitrogen** requirements. Refer to "Lawn Maintenance Made Easy" on page 51 for specifics.

JUNE

Mow and water—but only as needed. Watch for changes in your lawn. If it changes from green to yellow, that means it's entering **semidormancy**. Don't worry—this is normal! You shouldn't try to revive it by watering or fertilizing. Your grass will come back in the fall—it's only resting.

Also, examine your lawn for clues about your soil. For instance, clover is a sign that

Cool-Season Grasses   **Warm-Season Grasses**

your soil lacks sufficient **nitrogen**. (See "Sizing Up Your Lawn" on page 9 for more clues.)

Continue to **mow and water** as necessary. Make mowing easier on yourself by **resharpening** your mower blades. Bahiagrass especially requires sharp blades. **Plug or sod** bare areas.

JULY

Sharpen your mower blades—yes, again! A sharp blade causes less stress to the grass. Besides, your lawn is growing so slowly that you can mow as infrequently as every three weeks (especially if the weather is dry), so you'll have plenty of time to devote to sharpening.

Continue to **mow and water** your lawn as necessary.

AUGUST

Test your soil, especially if you think your lawn needs help. How much topsoil do you have? Check and see: 4 inches is good—6 is better. (See page 9 for tips on investigating your soil.)

Continue mowing, but only as needed.

Make a second application of **organic fertilizer**. If you're waiting for plugs or sprigs to fill in your lawn, get out the hoe and take care of any **weeds** that are filling in faster than your grass. **Mow and water** as necessary.

SEPTEMBER

This is a busy month! Look at all you can be doing to care for your lawn:

- If your lawn has bare spots, **seed** them now.

- If your lawn is sparse or if you'd like to overseed with a pest- or disease-resistant grass species, **reseed** now.

- **Spread organic fertilizer** or a thin layer of sieved compost.

- And of course, **mow and water as necessary** as your grass is actively growing.

Don't stop now! **Continue to mow and water** as necessary.

OCTOBER

If your soil test indicated that you need to raise the pH, **add lime**. If your pH is too high, consider

adding sulfur. Mow only as needed; the growing season is nearly over.

Warm-season grasses are entering dormancy, and you can begin to **slow down**, too. Cease irrigation as the growth stops.

NOVEMBER

Mow over fallen leaves to chop them up. **Rake** the chopped leaves if the cover is very thick (for example, under a Norway or sugar maple) and save them to use next spring as mulch. Often you can get away with just leaving them on the lawn, where they'll decompose and add nutrients. When you mow for the last time this season, mow your lawn shorter than usual.

Test your soil to determine **pH and soil deficiencies**. Then take a break from lawn care!

DECEMBER

Zzzzzzzzzzzzzzzz. Whether you grow cool- or warm-season grass, **your lawn is resting, so you can, too!**

Lawn-Care Glossary

Learning the lawn-care lingo will make your trips to the home and garden center easier. Here's a list of terms you're likely to come across in this book as well as in the grass seed or fertilizer aisles.

Aeration. Boring holes in the soil with a special tool or a spading fork to open up spaces in it so that oxygen, water, and nutrients can reach grass roots. It is generally ineffective and unnecessary in a healthy lawn, although it may help lawns growing in heavy clay soil.

Clay soil. Soil that is made up of very fine particles that hold nutrients well but are poorly drained. Clay soil is heavy and difficult to work.

Compost. Decomposed and partially decomposed organic matter that is dark in color and crumbly in texture. Used as an amendment, compost increases the water-holding capacity and drainage of the soil and is an excellent nutrient source for microorganisms, which later release nutrients to your plants.

Cool-season grass. Any grass species that grows well in spring and fall (such as Kentucky bluegrass or fescue) but grows slowly or goes into a dormant state in the heat of summer.

Dethatching. Removal of excessive thatch with a dethatching machine or rake. Thatch buildup is caused by overfertilization, which can result in lawn grass growing at a faster rate than the soil organisms can break it down, and by the use of pesticides that kill earthworms, important decomposers of thatch. With good organic lawn-care practices, most lawns shouldn't need dethatching.

Endophyte. A naturally occurring fungus that lives inside some grass plants. It doesn't harm the grass, and endophyte-infected grasses are more resistant to insects and have better drought tolerance. *Note:* Endophytes are harmful to livestock, so don't plant endophyte-infected grasses in grazing areas.

Fertilizer. A natural or manufactured material added to the soil that supplies one or more of the major nutrients (nitrogen, phosphorus, and potassium) to growing plants.

Foliar feeding. A way to give grass a light nutrient boost by spraying plants with a liquid fertilizer that is absorbed through the leaf pores. Compost tea and seaweed extract are two examples of organic foliar lawn fertilizers.

Grubs. Larvae of beetles and other insects that overwinter in the soil, feeding on grass roots early and late in the season. You can recognize grubs by their white, C-shaped bodies; control them with milky disease spore.

Herbicide. A substance used to kill unwanted plants. Some types are selective (they kill only a certain type of plant); others are nonselective and will kill any plants they come in contact with. Corn gluten meal is one of the very few effective organic herbicides.

Humus. A dark-colored, stable form of organic matter that remains after most of the plant and animal residues in it have decomposed.

Hydroseeding. Establishing a lawn area by spraying a slurry, which is a mixture of grass seed, fertilizer, fiber mulch, and water.

Loam. The best texture of soil to have. It contains a balance of fine clay, medium-size silt, and coarse sand particles. Loam is easily tilled and retains moisture and nutrients effectively.

Named variety. A subdivision of a plant species that has been selected for its improved vigor, fine texture, or other desirable characteristics and then bred and named by the industry to ensure a standard of quality.

Nematodes. Microscopic, slender, translucent roundworms, many of which act beneficially as decomposers and pest parasites. Other nematodes feed on and damage plant roots.

Nitrogen. An element that promotes vigorous growth and healthy color and is one of the three main nutrients in a complete fertilizer. Plants can't use nitrogen directly from the air—it's converted naturally by soil microbes into a form that plants can absorb.

NPK. A recognized abbreviation that refers to the ratio of the three major nutrients—nitrogen (N), phosphorus (P), and potassium (K)—in fertilizer, such as 5-5-5 or 10-2-2.

Organic. Materials that are derived directly from plants or animals. Organic gardening uses plant and animal by-products to maintain soil and plant health and doesn't rely on synthetically made fertilizers, herbicides, or pesticides.

Overseeding. Renewing a lawn area by sowing seeds over an existing lawn without first clearing away existing sod. Overseeding is used to spruce up a weary lawn or to introduce disease-resistant grasses or a different grass species.

Pesticide. Any substance, synthetic or natural, which is used to kill insects, animals, fungi, bacteria, or weeds.

pH. A measure of how acidic or alkaline a substance is. The pH scale ranges from 1 to 14, with 7 indicating neutrality, below 7 acidity, and above 7 alkalinity. The pH of your soil has a great effect on what nutrients are available to your plants.

Plugs. Small pieces of sod of creeping types of grasses, or seedlings or cuttings of a groundcover. Plugs are generally planted 6 to 12 inches apart, depending upon how quickly they will grow together to cover an area.

Sandy soil. Soil that contains more than 70 percent sand and less than 15 percent clay. Sandy soil is usually well drained and easy to work with, but it has poor nutrient- and water-holding abilities.

Silt. Soil particles of moderate size—larger than clay but smaller than sand.

Sod. Strips of living grass held together by matted roots that can be laid on a prepared soil bed to create an instant lawn.

Soil test kit. A set of instructions and a soil bag available through your state's Cooperative Extension Service. Test results indicate soil pH and specify what amendments and nutrients should be added to your soil to ensure success with your planned use.

Spreader. A bin on wheels with an adjustable opening for spreading grass seed, fertilizer, or amendments evenly, usually over a lawn. Drop spreaders drop seed and fertilizer directly on the ground as you push them; broadcast spreaders spew the material in a radius up to 10 feet from the spreader.

Thatch. A layer consisting of the roots, stolons, and rhizomes of grass plants that fail to decompose. Thatch can accumulate to excess if the lawn has been overfertilized, or if earthworm populations have been reduced by the use of pesticides.

Topdressing. Covering the lawn surface with a thin layer of a soil amendment, such as finely screened compost, to improve or maintain soil health.

Transition zone. The geographical area where both warm- and cool-season grasses will grow, but where neither type is at its best.

Turfgrass. Grass varieties selected and bred for best performance as lawn grasses.

VNS. On a package or grass seed, VNS stands for "variety not stated" and indicates unspecified varieties of lawn seed. Grass grown from VNS seed is inconsistent in quality.

Warm-season grass. Any species of grass, such as bermudagrass or zoysiagrass, that grows well in summer, even in hot, dry climates, and is usually dormant in winter.

Weeds. Any plants that happen to grow where you don't want them to. Some perfectly fine plants can be considered weeds when they pop up in the wrong places.

Recommended Reading & Resources

Books & Periodicals

Carr, Anna, et al. *Rodale's Chemical-Free Yard and Garden.* Emmaus, PA: Rodale, 1991.

Daniels, Stevie. *The Wild Lawn Handbook: Alternatives to the Traditional Front Lawn.* New York: Macmillan Publishing Co., 1995.

Ellis, Barbara. *Safe and Easy Lawn Care: The Complete Guide to Organic, Low-Maintenance Lawns.* (Taylor's Weekend Gardening Guide Series.) Boston: Houghton Mifflin Co., 1997.

Franklin, Stuart. *Building a Healthy Lawn: A Safe and Natural Approach.* Pownal, VT: Storey Communications, 1988.

Hill, Lewis, and Nancy Hill. *Rodale's Successful Organic Gardening: Lawns, Grasses, and Groundcovers.* Emmaus, PA: Rodale, 1995.

Raymond, Dick. *Down-to-Earth Natural Lawn Care.* Pownal, VT: Storey Communications, 1993.

Schultz, Warren. *The Chemical-Free Lawn.* Emmaus, PA: Rodale, 1989.

Walheim, Lance, et al. *Lawn Care for Dummies.* Foster City, CA: IDG Books Worldwide, 1998.

Woodson, R. Dodge. *Watering Systems for Lawn and Garden.* Pownal, VT: Storey Communications, 1996.

Organic Gardening magazine. Rodale, 33 East Minor Street, Emmaus, PA 18098.

Tools & Supplies

A. M. Leonard, Inc.
241 Fox Drive
Piqua, Ohio 45356-0816
Phone: (800) 543-8955
Fax: (800) 543-0633
E-mail: info@amleo.com
Web site: www.amleo.com

Gardener's Supply Company
128 Intervale Road
Burlington, VT 05401
Phone: (800) 863-1700
Fax: (800) 551-6712
E-mail: info@gardeners.com
Web site: www.gardeners.com

Gardens Alive!
5100 Schenley Place
Lawrenceburg, IN 47025
Phone: (812) 537-8650
Fax: (812) 537-5108
E-mail: gardener@gardens-alive.com
Web site: www.gardens-alive.com

Harmony Farm Supply
3244 Gravenstein Highway North
Sebastopol, CA 95472
Phone: (707) 823-9125
Fax: (707) 823-1734
E-mail: info@harmonyfarm.com
Web site: www.harmonyfarm.com

Peaceful Valley Farm Supply
P.O. Box 2209
Grass Valley, CA 95945
Phone: (530) 272-4769
Fax: (530) 272-4794
E-mail: contact@groworganic.com
Web site: www.groworganic.com

Acknowledgments

Contributors to this book include Christine Bucks, Anna Carr, Mike Ferrara, Cheryl Long, Scott Meyer, Lon Rombough, Paul Sachs, and Warren Schultz.

Photo Credits

Matthew Benson vi, 3, 5, 7, 11 (bottom), 38, 50, 52, 53, 55, 57, 59, 62, 63, 89

Deneeve Feigh Bunde/Unicorn Stock 91

Rob Cardillo 46, 47, 96, 97

J. C. Carlton/Bruce Coleman Stock 74

David Cavagnaro 69 (top), 70 (top), 82

Walter Chandoha 15, 67 (top), 83 (top)

Betty Crowell 26 (bottom), 35 (top), 73 (bottom)

Alan and Linda Detrick 10 (bottom), 70 (bottom)

Tom Edwards/Unicorn Stock 12

Derek Fell i, 23 (top), 83 (bottom), 84, 87

Jane Grushow/Grant Heilman Photography 94

Sunniva Hart/Garden Picture Library 88

judywhite/New Leaf Images 20 (both), 21 (middle and bottom), 22 (both), 23 (bottom)

R. Kopfle/Bruce Coleman Stock 8

Dwight Kuhn 71

Kit Latham 31 (bottom), 32, 34, 35 (bottom), 36

Holly Lynton 14 (top)

Mitch Mandel 2, 13, 14 (bottom), 16, 40, 41, 42, 43, 44, 45, 47, 49, 61

Charles Mann 86

Bert McCarty/Clemson University 72 (both), 73 (top)

John Peden 78

Photo Alto 4

Barbara Pleasant 68 (bottom), 69 (bottom)

Hans Reinhard/Bruce Coleman Stock 80

Maria Rodale 64

Susan A. Roth iv, 21 (top)

Barry Runk/Grant Heilman Photography 67 (bottom), 68 (top)

Spectrum Stock 8

Jim Strawser/Grant Heilman Photography 60

Michael S. Thompson 10 (top), 11 (top), 26 (top), 27, 28, 31 (top), 48, 85, 93

Terry Wilde 24

Index

F

Fairy rings, 73, *73*
Fences, planting along, 95
Fertilizers, organic
    applying, 54–56, 58
    vs. chemical, 2–3, *2*, 57, *57*
    nitrogen content, by type, **58**
Fescues. *See* Fine fescues; Tall fescues
Fine fescues
    characteristics of, 21, *21*, 61, 75
    diseases prone to, 72–73
    mowing height for, 53
    zones for, 18–19
Fungi
    beneficial, 75
    harmful, 73, *73*

G

Garden forks, *38*, 39, *46*, 47,
    62–63, *63*
Glossary, lawn-care, 98–99
Grape hyacinth, 93
Grass clippings
    leaving on lawn, 3, 6, 53–54, 56
    removing from lawn, 54, *55*
Grasses. *See also specific grasses*
    cool-season, 17–18, 20–21, *20, 21*
    drought-tolerant, 61
    endophytic, 75
    nitrogen needs of, by type, **56**
    roots of, 4
    warm-season, 17–18, 22–23, *22, 23*
    zones for, 18–19
Groundcovers
    choosing, 79–80
    coverage from, 86
    erosion mats for, 89, *89*
    vs. lawns, 6–7, 80
    profiles of, 81–85
Ground ivy, 68, *68*
Grubs, 11–12, *12*, 74–75

H

Heat stress, 58
Herbicides, 4, 66
Herb lawns, 86–89

Hoses, 39, 48
Hostas, 83
Hydroseeding, 32, *32*

I

Insects
    beneficial, 66
    pests, 4, 75, **76–77**
Ivy. *See* English ivy; Ground ivy

J

Junipers, 84

K

Kentucky bluegrass
    characteristics of, 20, *20*, 61
    diseases prone to, 72–73
    in seed mixes, 30
    watering, 59
    zones for, 18–19

L

Labels, seed, 28–30, *29*
Lady's-mantle, 82, *83*
Lamium, spotted, 79
Lawn maintenance. *See also* Fertilizers,
    organic; Mowing; Watering
    calendar for, 96–97
    hiring service for, 52
    for new lawns, 36–37
    organic vs. traditional, 1–7
    terms, defined, 98–99
Lawn rollers, 28, *28*
Leaves, on lawns, 55
Lilyturfs, 82
Lime, 15, *15*
Lobelia, great blue, 92

M

Magnesium, 15
Maiden pinks, 83, *83*
Maintenance. *See* Lawn maintenance;
    Mowers, maintenance of
Meadows, wildflower, 90–92, *91*
Mints, 88–89
Moles, 74–75, *74*

Mosses, 11
Moss pinks, 79
Mother-of-thyme, 79
Mowers
    as essential, 39
    maintenance of, 42, *42,* 44, 53
    reel, 41, 43–44, *43*
    riding, 44, *44*
    walk-behind, 40–42, *40, 41*
Mowing
    cutting patterns, *52*
    height for, 5–6, *5,* 52–53, *53*
    meadows, 92
    new lawns, 37
    schedules for, 51–52
Mowing strips, *94,* 95
Mulch
    vs. lawns, *7,* 95
    for new lawns, 31, *31,* 81, 92

N
Nitrogen
    from grass clippings, 6, 53, 54
    in organic fertilizers, **58**
    requirements, by grass type, **56**
    weeds and, 10

O
Overseeding
    appropriateness of, 25
    technique, 32–34
    to fight pests, 75
Overwatering, 5, 61
Oxeye daisy, 90

P
Pachysandra
    Japanese, 85
    planting, to prevent ground ivy, 68
Pennyroyal, 88
Peppermint, 89
Perennial ryegrass. *See also* Ryegrass,
    annual
    vs. annual, 30
    characteristics of, 20, *20,* 61, 75
    overseeding with, 33

in seed mixes, 30
    zones for, 18–19
Periwinkle, 82, *82,* 85
Pesticides, 3–4, 75
Pests
    insects, 4, 75, **76–77**
    rodents, 74–75, 95
pH level, of soil, 13, 27
Pink thread, *73*
Pitch forks. *See* Garden forks
Plaintain, broadleaf, 11, 67, *67*
Purple coneflower, 92

Q
Quackgrass, 70, *70*
Queen-Anne's-lace, 90

R
Rakes, *38,* 39, 46–47, *46, 62*
Red fescue, 21, *21,* 30, 72–73
Red thread, 73, *73*
Redtop, 72
Regions, climatic, 18–19
Reseeding. *See* Overseeding
Rodents, 74–75, *74*
Roots, 4
Rosemary, 88
Ryegrass, annual, 30, 33, 61, 72–73.
    See also Perennial ryegrass

S
Seaweed, liquid, 58, 73
Seed
    labels on, 28–30, *29*
    mixes of, 29–30
    vs. sod, 26, *26*
    starting lawn from, 30–34, *31, 32,* 36
Shade, lawn alternatives in, 81–82, 84–85, 95
Shovels, *38,* 39, 46, *46*
Skunks, 75
Slice seeders, 33
Slugs, 70
Snowdrops, common, 93
Sod
    buying, 34, 36
    laying, *34,* 35–36, *35, 36*

USDA Plant Hardiness Zone Map

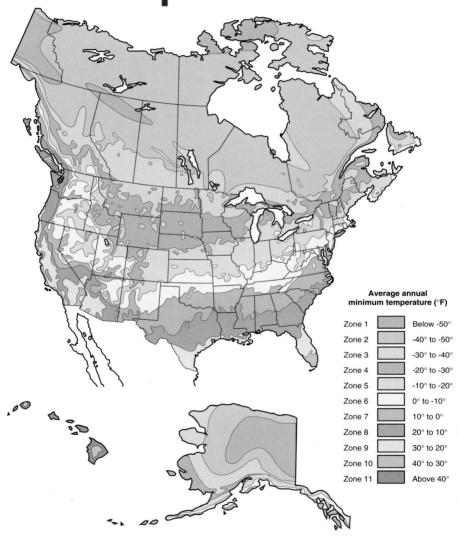

**Average annual
minimum temperature (°F)**

Zone 1		Below -50°
Zone 2		-40° to -50°
Zone 3		-30° to -40°
Zone 4		-20° to -30°
Zone 5		-10° to -20°
Zone 6		0° to -10°
Zone 7		10° to 0°
Zone 8		20° to 10°
Zone 9		30° to 20°
Zone 10		40° to 30°
Zone 11		Above 40°

This map was revised in 1990 and is recognized as the best indicator of minimum temperatures available. Look at the map to find your area, then match its color to the key at the right. When you've found your color, the key will tell you what hardiness zone you live in. Remember that the map is a general guide; your particular conditions may vary.